Changing Mindsets & Developing Spirit

Inspirational Coaching through Verse for Success in Sport & Life

By Helen K Emms

To Wendy (Troll)
with love
Helen x
October 2010

l!p

First published in 2010 by:

Live It Publishing
27 Old Gloucester Road
London, United Kingdom.
WC1N 3AX
www.liveitpublishing.com

All enquiries should be addressed to Live It Publishing.
ISBN 978-1-906954-07-9 (pbk)

Dedication

To the choices we make that
determine who we become.

May we choose wisely and
live every moment in gratitude

For our Life.

Contents

Introduction

Welcome to *Changing Mindsets & Developing Spirit*. A book of personal coaching through verse. I have written this book to inspire you to be the best that you can be. We all have many talents, our mission in life is to recognise them and then realise our talent. In my view, a wasted talent is a waste of life and the only true failure is not realising the talent you have; not striving to be the best you can be. Through my experience as a Personal Development Coach, working with a wide range of people in sports, career and life, it is very clear to me that the one thing that stops us all being as successful as we can is fear. Whether that fear is of failure, not being good enough, not being accepted or not loved makes no difference, it is still fear and it will always hold you back.

The antidote to fear is your *Spiritual Self*, which is that part of you that has faith in yourself and what you can achieve in life. When you feel inspired, have belief and faith in yourself, you feel you can achieve anything you set your mind to. You may have had glimpses of this part of you, through; your intuition, your creativity, your ideas, visions and dreams, your sense of knowing something is right, your experiences of connectedness to others and nature. Fear causes us to think in specific ways, from which we create mindsets that do not support our desires and potential. In writing this book I want to help you to develop effective mindsets and connect with your *Spiritual Self*, in order to be the best that you can be, in whatever you choose to do in your life. The verses are intended to provoke your thinking, overcome your current mindsets, inspire you to become aware of how great you really are, help you feel comforted that you are not alone in your struggle, provide guidance and support, and generally raise your awareness to your inner struggle to live as your *Self*. Through this process you will begin to fully utilize the power of your mind and tap into the essence of who you are: your *Spiritual Self*.

Throughout this book you will come to appreciate that your natural, perhaps innate, tendencies as Human beings, to be defensive, hide from failure, blame, seek vengeance, strive or even fight for more or better, to judge others, feel inferior or superior to others, and much more, can be overcome. The whole premise behind the fact that we adopt mindsets is in the very word; they can be 'set' and therefore difficult to change. However, we can learn to change our mindsets, become more accepting, forgiving, gracious, loving, joyful, sharing and connected and through doing so enjoy our sporting, career and life experiences as they were intended. No longer do you need to beat yourself up when you don't do as well as you wanted, no longer do you need to put yourself down or build yourself up. But what you do need to do, is recognize your innate talents, whether god given or not, and appreciate all the ways in which you can fully achieve your potential. You need to become familiar with the idea that you are already good enough, you are already perfect. Change can only take place within you, and throughout this book you will be directed to change your thinking, mental processing and interpretation of things, such that you free yourself up to achieve your highest potential. Achieving your potential is not, however, a purely thought driven act, it is one that emanates through your *Spiritual Self* and utilizes all your emotions. In fact, it is often the case that your thinking can seriously limit your achievement of your highest potential as you will come to realize, if you haven't already!

The book is divided by sections and each section is explained before providing you with some key coaching points and verse to help you to experience and develop a new understanding. As you read, there may be ideas you come across that initially you may feel you don't relate to. If this is the case, please be assured that with time, repetition, and perhaps undertaking further reading, you will become more familiar with the ideas, see their significance in what you do and undertake to change your perspective in order to achieve what you want in your life.

You can read this book any way you wish, either from start to finish or dipping in to the areas or specific verse that appeals to you. The more often you read, the easier change will be. Although some verses are written to illustrate the experiences within a sporting environment, you will easily be able to read them with a broader interpretation and find that they apply to your experiences in other areas of your life. After all, we are all here playing the game of life right now! For example, you can think of winning or losing, getting things right or wrong, planning, taking actions, self deprecating thoughts, striving, failing, succeeding, etc in many aspects of your life. In fact, the reality is simply that, whatever you bring to your sport or career, is a reflection of your life. Whichever way you approach your reading, I hope that you enjoy your experience, feel comforted that you are not alone, feel supported, guided and inspired and begin to fully realise that you have everything you need to achieve the best you can in whatever you desire.

Helen K Emms
Buckinghamshire, UK
January 2010

This Life Is All We Have

This life we live is all we have,
Whilst mortal on this land,
Although your Spirit will last forever,
Your physical *Self* is earth bound.

Make the most of all you have,
In your current state,
For you only get one chance to live,
And it's never too late.

Live the life you want to live,
Don't keep living in the past,
Don't wait for life to come to you,
Your time will go too fast.

Your life is yours to live with joy,
Find out who you really are,
Live now as you want your future to be,
No pain to leave its scar.

It's Difficult to Change

"It's difficult" are words I often hear,
When changing mindsets and thoughts,
"That's right" I say, it's tough to change,
The habits of a lifetime.

The way we think is precious to us,
We may even think it's fixed,
It's not, it's just so well engrained,
And easier to live with than to change.

Even though my thinking doesn't help,
It makes me feel more stressed,
It's what I know, so comfortable,
So I'll get what I get, I'm not blessed.

But you can change, everyone can,
It requires just a little effort, and to repeat,
And trust there's a better place out there,
Have courage to walk a new street.

Changing Perspectives

Changing perspectives is as good a place to start this book as any because very simply, that is what life is about. Wherever there is miscommunication between people there will be different perspectives. Wherever you experience inner conflict, there will be different perspectives at play. In an absolute sense, no perspective is either right or wrong; it simply is as it is. How do we create our perspective? We experience the world through our senses, each of which operates via a "spectrum", which is a form of measurement. Our visual and auditory senses are experienced through a range of frequencies. Even our thoughts are transmitted at different frequencies, with positive thoughts at higher frequencies and negative thoughts at lower frequencies. The frequencies that we are tuned into are different from many other species on the planet. Even within the Human species, our sensory experiences will be different. For example, artists see things differently from others, musicians hear things differently from others, healers feel things differently than others and those who judge the quality of food and wine have a different gustatory and olfactory experience than others. Whilst it is easy to appreciate these differences, we often forget and subsequently label people, such as psychics, as "odd", "wacky" or some other descriptive term that implies they are either false or strange. Our perspectives are also determined through our knowledge, age, cultural and social norms and other "rules" that we have been taught to be "true" or "right". If we can easily lose sight of the fact that other people may have a different sensory experience to us, when it comes to thoughts, beliefs and values we are even more stubborn in not accepting such differences as equally right, valid and true as our own.

Your evaluation of what you have done in life, will be from a specific perspective, such as: the perspective that you should be doing better, you should be perfect, you should be able to achieve this or that, easily. Our perspectives are therefore driven by our interpretation of what we have experienced through our senses. To change our perspective we may or may not be able to change the range at which we can sense the world, but we can change our mental interpretation, which would lead us to then experience the same sensory event differently. Most people's objections to this idea come from the fact that they believe what they perceive to be true. This is technically incorrect. What you have experienced is a sensory event and "your interpretation" of what has happened is driven by your internal thoughts and emotional processing; your values, beliefs, memories, personal characteristics and so on.

Seeing something from another's perspective is essentially stepping into their shoes and seeing things as they are seeing them. In the relationship between an athlete and their coach, very often the athlete will have a different perspective on what they have done, or are doing, than the coach. It really helps athletes to develop when both parties are able to understand each others perspectives and also then agree on the direction the development should be taken. They will then be "singing from the same hymn sheet", "talking the same language" and communication will be effective and feel easy. The same is true of course for any and all relationships. If you disagree with someone, it is most likely that their interpretation of events (their perspective) is simply different from yours.

Key Coaching Points:

Here are some thoughts to help you accept the perspectives of others:

* Respect another's perspective, knowing that if you were them your perspective would be the same as theirs.

* You don't need to agree with another to respect their different views.

* Just because someone has a different perspective doesn't make you, or them, wrong.

* The world would be a very boring place if everyone saw things the same way.

Different Views

How can you see a different view,
When what you see feels so true?
How can you think of other ways,
When the one you have feels it's here to stay?

There are different ways to see,
What has happened and what might be.
Just look through another's mind,
A different interpretation there to find.

It's not about what's right or wrong,
It's simply about what helps you along.
If your view just holds you back,
Think again and change tack.

You have to allow yourself to change,
The fixed ideas and beliefs you engage,
Look with another's attitude,
A new perspective you cannot elude.

Another Day

Another day, it didn't go great,
Nothing I can do, it's all too late.
Frustrated and angry, I don't want to review,
I should have won, what can I do?

I can watch with open eye,
Like the spaceman from the sky.
And know that I did my best,
Even if it wasn't as good as the rest.

Tomorrow I can try again,
And leave behind this awful pain.
Tomorrow is another day,
I can do things a different way.

Tomorrow is another chance,
My performance I can always enhance.
It's all about striving to improve,
With this attitude I can never lose.

Imagine

Imagine what you would do,
If you thought like me and not like you.
How would your world be,
If you saw your life like the sea?
All the wonders would you find there,
Buried treasures of which you are unaware.

Imagine all that you could do,
If you could see a different you.
How would your life expand,
If you saw yourself through God's hand?
All the achievements, the wonder of you,
Your true *Self* you would anew.

Don't see your life as black and white,
Know there's more than day and night.
You are not one thing or another,
No longer do you need to suffer.
Multi-dimensional, creative being,
Just open your eyes and start seeing.

The Spaceman

The spaceman who sees from the sky,
Looks through a very different eye,
Than the sailor on the ship,
Who is on the sea with all its rage,
Who sees the chopping wave.

The spaceman's view of the same,
Is calm, serene, a blue expanse,
No risk to take, or chance.

In the thick of stormy action,
It's impossible to not see trouble happening.

But through the spaceman's eye, far away,
Is the only way to judge your day.

All your actions that didn't go well,
Will appear like the sea in the spacemen's spell.

From that distance nothing is that bad,
And there is no reason to feel sad.

Observe Don't Think

To be aware is not to think,
The two are very different.
Awareness involves the senses,
Thinking is a processing state.
When aware, you are the observer,
When you are thinking, you are the thought.
Awareness keeps you above the mire,
Thinking can make you feel distraught.
You must be aware of what you have done,
And you must think about your plan.
But ensure when things go off track,
Your thoughts don't dominate and attack.
Stay the observer, aware of it all,
Rise above, don't allow yourself to fall.
Trust yourself to respond as planned,
Stay calm, composed, keep your mind in hand.
You will come through,
You always do.
It's better to watch, and stay aware,
Than get stuck in thought, running scared.

The Wise Man Says

The wise man would see you a different way,
The wise man sees all shades of grey.
One day we can be this, and then that,
The shades of grey are never flat.

Options and potential is who you are,
Change in your nature, your destiny is far.
Fear is all that stops you through,
Your fixed ideas of what is true.

But when we are allowed to change,
Our mind, our heart, to rearrange.
You have to be aware of what's really true,
The laws of the universe are but a few.

Thoughts and ideas are transient notions,
What we achieve, the feel of our emotions.
When we see them as wrong or right,
Changing perspectives will always be a fight.

Thinking & Thought Control

It is believed that we have in excess of 50,000 thoughts per day and I am sure most of you can relate to this with the constant stream of thoughts running through your head. Some thoughts are related to what you are doing in any moment, but many seem to be completely out of context. Now, ask yourself, how many of your thoughts are positive, encouraging, supportive and enabling, and how many are negative, destructive, critical or disabling?

It seems very easy for your mind to wander off in any moment, triggered by some sensory experience or another, but completely off track! There you were, in conversation, or the middle of a sporting activity and your mind has gone somewhere completely different. So when we talk about 'thought control' it can feel like a contradiction in terms. In fact, the word 'control' is inappropriate when talking about thoughts, because it doesn't feel as if we control them coming into our head, which, initially, we don't because they are formed from habit. It might, therefore help to think of 'directing' or 'reigning in' thoughts, or 'observing' them.

The constant stream of thoughts you experience, and the type of thought you engage in can be changed, but it requires effort to do so. It requires you to recognize your thoughts for what they are: your internal verbal dialogue, driven by your desire to know how the world works, your instinctive drive to identify problems and your subsequent analysis of your experiences in any moment. To turn off your thoughts you need to turn off your natural desire to label, critique, evaluate, analyse, problem solve, investigate, and you need to turn off your fear that something out there is going to get you! Instead you need to learn to simply observe, without that internal commentary, create a space between your thoughts, chill out a bit and let go of your need to control. People spend years perfecting this behaviour and I am not suggesting you need to go that far, but in order to be able to achieve your highest potential, you need to learn to create this no-thinking state. This no-thinking state is also relevant for those who are performing in any context; e.g. on stage, presenting, a musician and so forth.

At any moment there are appropriate thoughts to have and there are inappropriate thoughts. The inappropriate thoughts are simply distractions. All your thoughts are therefore directly linked to your concentration. Thinking is one of the biggest, if not the only, distraction in the sporting context and life. It takes your attention away from the most important thing in that moment – the task you are performing, the 'now'. Any form of *Self* criticism is therefore not helpful; it is both a distraction and has a negative effect on your confidence. Although many people think that it is necessary to be critical, it is a false belief. There is a big difference between being aware of what you have done and being critical of yourself. Any form of thought distraction will have an impact on your body and subsequently your performance. Thought distractions also impact your emotional state, again affecting your performance.

It is important to understand the difference between thinking, awareness and intention, since these are "thought behaviours" that create a very different effect on your ability to perform. The term thinking captures the 'processing' aspects of the mind, actively engaged in mentally appreciating what is happening; labelling, evaluating, criticizing, judging and may have an emotive expression, i.e. a value judgment, such as being positive or negative, right or wrong. Awareness is a state of observing, watching without judgment or evaluation, just noticing what is happening. There is no emotional expression, since no value judgment is being made. For example, I can be aware that it is snowing outside today and have no further mental input to that. However, if I notice that it is snowing and then make a judgment about that being a good or bad thing, make comments about the type of snow etc, then I am in thinking mode. My thinking can be emotive or factual. Having an intention is like taking a decision. It is setting your mind to do something and is a very powerful pre-framing tool that you have, which means if you set your intention it is more likely to happen than if you don't because you have effectively 'told yourself' that you are going to do it. Many people set intentions at the New Year, called resolutions. Some intentions can be very strong, with high levels of determination and motivation to make them happen, such as intending to go on holiday, and some intentions can be weak, as in some New Year's resolutions that last for only a month.

Within sport, we would set intentions in terms of our plans, for example, our development plan and also our tactical plan for the performance. You can set an intention to remain calm during the game. You can set an intention to behave in a specific way if something doesn't go to plan. In setting these intentions they are more likely to happen than if you don't set them. Any evaluations and mental processing should be as objective (factual) as possible and therefore without a value judgment. Awareness is essential for development. You cannot change what you are not aware of. The process of raising your awareness can also be a painful one, as you realise your faults and areas for improvement. This can be especially painful in respect of changing mindsets; thought patterns, emotional responses and interpretations, since we are often more attached to our thoughts than we are to our physical skill development.

Thinking is necessary and there are effective thoughts and less effective thoughts. You have the power to change your thoughts, but you have to put in effort and be determined to change. You are going to need to break down old habitual ways of thinking. These ways have served you, to a point, but they have not always helped you to achieve your highest potential. The main reason for this is that many of the thoughts you have will keep you within your comfort zone, a place that is safe, rather than push you into a place of discomfort and uncertainty. Even though you may not get the results you want with your current thinking patterns, there is a stronger drive in you to be safe than to change. That doesn't make change impossible, but like anything that is worth something in life, you have to have the desire to put in effort and the self-discipline; to never quit. Effort and self-discipline are qualities that are essential to you developing your *Spiritual Self*.

Key Coaching Points:

* ❋ Your thoughts, whether good or bad, become your reality.

* ❋ Think only that which supports you and do not give energy to that which doesn't.

* ❋ Thinking is optional, what you think is a choice.

* ❋ Your thoughts are old habits, check they still apply before following them!

* ❋ Awareness doesn't guarantee change but a lack of awareness guarantees you won't change.

* ❋ Be determined, set your intention, then deliver what you intended and don't let habitual thinking stop you.

* ❋ When you think about something you don't want you make that thing more likely to happen.

* ❋ Your thoughts are not true, but they make up your reality, and that makes them true for you.

* The biggest mistake you can make is to believe what you think is true.

* Hold on to the thoughts that help you and let go of the ones that don't – it's called selective thinking.

* Your thoughts create your own reality, make sure it's the reality you want!

Thinking Is Necessary

It's easier not to not think,
When I think it all goes wrong.
Yet I know I should be thinking something,
But when I think it just gets worse.
Maybe there's a time and a place,
To think and not to think,
So it doesn't stop me playing well,
And doesn't keep me in the bad habit spell.

There is a time to think, it's in between,
The phases of the game.
It isn't being critical or technical,
It's on what you want to achieve.
It's tactical and understanding,
What you need to do and believe.
To beat the skills of the other player,
Take advantage of their weakness,
Utilise your strengths,
It's physical chess you're engaged in.
So think about your strategy,
Don't get caught up in your errors,
Keep your thoughts on what you want to do,
Then thinking can't go wrong for you.

Positive Self Talk

When I say "come on" to me,
It gives me hope I might succeed.
When I say "oh no what's wrong",
I have lost hope, my game is gone.

When I say "let's go",
I feel on my toes.
When I say "this isn't working",
Failure is lurking.

So even when it's not going well,
I must create a positive spell.
Say good things to help my game,
And stop looking for things to blame.

Being positive will come true,
But you have to believe in you.
If you doubt you make it tough,
And playing well is always rough.

Letting Go

People talk of letting go,
To get into the flow,
But how do they know?
It should be so easy to do,
Maybe it is for you.

I get tight and think about a lot,
Seems like these thoughts I cannot stop,
But how can it be?
Can I be free, if,
This is just me.

Letting go is an art,
You can easily start,
To stop believing your mind's chatter.
Your mind will always play tricks on you,
To hold on tight to what it thinks is true.

Letting go feels so false to me,
Because of all my thoughts running free,
When I do it feels like I don't care.
Yet, holding on is to sabotage my success,
What do I need to do to control the mess?

Letting go is to relax the tension,
Letting go is of another dimension,
It's an ongoing skill to develop.
Where tricks of the mind cannot harm you,
With confidence high you trust you will come through.

Letting go is about having faith,
Trust in your deeper *Self*,
Letting go of control of that which you cannot.
It's simply watching the thoughts in your mind,
Not allowing the illusion of failure to blind.

Letting go is realizing you are good enough,
It's seeing that your baggage is not really your stuff.
It's recognizing what really matters in life,
It's about being present now, being free,
It's simply about loving being me.

Self Control

Distraction is easy to do,
It requires no *Self* control.
It is the root of excuses too,
To help you get through.
Distraction eases the pain of failure,
Holding you back from fully committing.
But that's an illusion of the mind,
To have you feel better for a short time.
But there is nothing worse for your Soul,
Than not putting in all that you can.
You will never grow strong in Spirit,
While you cheat yourself to ease the pain.
Own up, take charge, control your *Self*,
Stay focussed on what you want.
Give it all until you have nothing left to give,
And then stop and feel content.

Tricks of the Mind

The mind plays tricks to keep us safe,
It will hold us back from achieving,
Frightened of our shadow,
Frightened of our loss,
Frightened that we are not good enough,
To achieve our dream.

Safety is its prime concern,
Your comfort zone, its hiding place,
To overcome these tricks of your mind,
You need to understand, be kind,
And step into the pain,
Rise to the challenge and gain,
The strength to carry on.

And no matter what you do or don't achieve,
You have nothing you need to prove,
Just fear to face and overcome,
Uncertainty to accept as fun,
Challenge something every day,
Your dream will come your way, so they say.

And accept the pain of failure,
That your heart will recover,
Stronger than before, and more,
Determined not to succumb,
To the tricks of the mind,
To have your comfort, keep you blind,
From the success that is in you to find.

I Don't Want To Think About It

I don't need to think during the game,
Just play and hope I'm not lame,
I'd rather think nothing and leave it to chance,
Hope luck is with me, making me dance.

Thinking distracts me,
Because I start to see,
The things I am doing wrong,
Then fear feels so strong.

When I think, there is such pain,
More comfortable for me to stay the same,
I feel better not thinking, calm and relaxed,
Until it goes wrong, then I collapse.

I have to think, because I do when I lose,
I need to learn to choose,
What thoughts to have and what to leave,
What I need to focus on, to achieve.

I must think to plan my approach,
Be my own, good coach,
Stay on my side and thinking smart,
Give myself the best start.

Plan to overcome problems along the way,
Leave nothing to chance that could ruin my day,
Positive I must remain,
Throughout the whole of the game.

Thinking is alright if you know what you are doing,
If you let your mind wander it can easily ruin,
Your chance of being the best you can be,
Thinking's alright when you do it like me.

Expect & You Shall Fail

When you expect and things go wrong,
How do you recover?
It should be this, it should be that,
It should be the other.

Expectations are fixed ways to think,
They have you feeling entitled,
So when they don't happen you just feel shattered,
It's unfair, it's wrong and it matters.

Instead set your sights high and just see what happens,
Work hard to achieve what you want,
Don't allow arrogance to get in the way,
Predicting your success today.

Try not to assess and get ahead of yourself,
It creates a false sense of confidence.
Know where you are and what you need to do,
To create success, take the setbacks and come through.

Negative Thought Control

My mind is such a power house,
Yet it feels so out of control,
Of all the thoughts that I have,
None help me at all.

Yet when I think,
It does come true,
Is it just me, or,
Is it like that for you?

I know I should be able to direct,
The thoughts in my head, so blue,
But being positive is hard because,
What if my good thoughts don't come true?

The only way that I can let go,
Of negative thoughts that haunt my mind,
Is bite the bullet and start to see,
All the positives I can find.

If I can see all the bad that's happening,
Then all the good is there too,
For one to exist so must the other,
It's just my perspective that's been skewed.

To see the positives just requires my effort,
And a desire to let go of the pain,
To praise my *Self*, for all the small things I achieve,
In my game and when I train.

Create a Space In Your Mind

I talk to myself all the time,
A constant voice in my head,
I'm not sure how to stop, if I could,
Or if I even really should.

The ideal state is to create a space,
Between the thoughts in your mind.
In this space you will see,
How good you can really be.

Thinking is most often distracting,
Criticizing my every action.
The space between my thoughts is free,
Of interference that stops me.

Create a space by watching your thoughts,
Just observe them from above,
Place each thought on a cloud,
Let them part and watch with love.

The space that you now create,
Just feels so great.
A softness in your mind appears,
Now you can perform so well, no fears.

Oh To Be Perfect

Oh to be perfect, what a delight,
No more striving, nothing to fight.
Oh when I am perfect, then what will I do,
I can feel good, never feel blue.

Oh to be perfect, what a joy to feel,
I've reached the end, satisfied by the meal.
Oh when I am perfect, then what will I do,
Nothing to achieve, nothing new.

And when I am perfect, the aching inside,
Will still reside,
The insecurity that I feel won't go away,
Even if I am perfect one day.

I am already perfect in the way that I can be,
I am a perfect Human, that's me!
What I do in life doesn't change the fact,
There's more to me and there's nothing I lack.

Ego Mind

We often think of the term Ego as associated with the macho ego, bravado style, generally linked to the male population. But, this is inaccurate. We all have an Ego and I want you to think of it as an energetic part of your mental functioning. If we were to think in opposites, we have the Ego and our *Spiritual Self*. There is a practical, survival aspect to the Ego. The Ego is also the responsible for your tendencies to: be competitive with others, need to feel better than others, a striving to improve and have more, and the attachment you have to your achievements as measures of your success as a Human being. All attributes found and even praised within the competitive sporting arena. Yet, these are also attributes that cause people to fail to achieve their highest potential, feel a failure, lack confidence, feel not good enough, give up, feel stressed and depressed and generally feel inadequate in life.

This attachment, which is a function of our Ego, is also what causes us to feel a sense of loss when something we are attached to is taken away from us. It is very easy to become attached to something when you have invested time and energy into it, and subsequently feel that your time has been wasted when you don't get out what you should do based on your investment. But this is an error in your thinking and can cause you to struggle to 'let go' and move on when it is necessary to do so. Detachment is the art of letting go of our Ego's attachment to things, ideas, thoughts, outcomes. Through detachment we are also letting go of the negative emotions such as sadness, guilt and anger that would be associated with loss. I should add here that detachment is not an absence of emotion; it is a separation of the '*Self*' from 'things'. It is the recognition that your identity (who you are) is not determined as a function of those 'things'; that you are more than your behaviours, achievements, acquisitions and thoughts.

It is the Ego part of our mental functioning that creates the illusion through which we live our lives. Many people object to the idea that we live our lives through illusion, but this is because they do not understand that our lives are a creation of our Ego Mind and therefore by the very nature our experiences must be an illusion. That doesn't make them intangible. The physical aspects of our experience exist. If someone steps on my foot, I feel the pain for sure. But the illusion happens when I make my interpretation of that event; I can imagine that the person did it deliberately in which case I will respond in a particular way, I can label them as clumsy and respond accordingly, or I can see it as an accident. Whichever way I interpret the situation becomes my reality, but that reality is an illusion of my imagination. Even labelling my experience as pain is part of the illusion.

The opposite, our *Spiritual Self,* is not about illusion. It is the part of us that experiences things as they are. It is the part of us that is infinite and immortal, intangible. Imagine, your thinking processes as primarily of your Ego Mind and your intuition being of your *Spiritual Self*. Very often you will override your intuition with your thinking processes, because you do not have the courage to trust your intuition and you too readily buy into the thinking processes of your Ego Mind as being an accurate representation of what you are experiencing. This situation, however, is changing, slowly, as people are becoming more familiar with and accepting that their intuition is an equally valid, and often more accurate, internal communication device than their thoughts.

Key Coaching Points:

⁕ If we choose to live with our illusions, we choose to feel the loss.

⁕ You cannot really lose what is not real and an illusion cannot be real.

⁕ Your Ego Mind is not real therefore you have nothing to lose.

⁕ Learn to follow your intuition not your thinking.

⁕ Let go of your idea that your thoughts are really what happened and see things for what they truly are... events, part of the game, not personal, not 'who I am'.

⁕ Who you are is much more than you think!

Ego Illusion

The ego force is strong in us,
It's drive for us to be better,
Than anyone else on the planet.
It isolates you,
From others it's true,
Just so you can feel special.
But it's a damaging force,
Although commonly linked,
With competitive desire in the game.
But the only true challenge,
Is the one that you have,
With your *Self*, your Soul and your name.
As soon as you realize,
The ego's illusion is to,
Keep you in comfort through fear.
You'll rise to the call,
Inside your Soul, and,
Ego will be gone, forever.

Ego Attachment

When my ego is strong,
The pain lasts so long,
I can't let go,
"I am" you know.

So stuck in this mind,
"What am I to do?"
When it doesn't work out,
I have to blame you.

Attached to my game,
The results that I get,
The illusion's the same,
I always win the bet.

Without my ego at play,
Nothing can be taken away,
Nothing to lose or feel sad about,
It feels so great, is all I can shout.

Feeling Misunderstood

It's easy to feel misunderstood,
Simple for you to maintain,
Separate yourself from the others,
Get stuck inside your brain.

Maintain the illusion through your thoughts,
Blame others for how you feel,
Yes, it's you that needs to feel so special,
Feeling misunderstood creates the appeal.

To not feel misunderstood,
Is really easy to achieve,
Talk, express, get your message through,
This isn't about anyone else, it's all about you.

The Illusion of Life

The game of life is a tricky thing,
Sometimes it makes you laugh and sing,
Another day you feel sad and cry,
Want to run away, escape, die.
But all of this a creation of the mind,
We are so blind,
Mind, so unkind.

The judgments that we make,
For our own sake,
Maintain the illusion of our success,
And the illusion of distress, a mess.
In judging others, we judge ourselves,
And create our own inner hell,
Under our own spell.

With love there really is no confusion,
We can easily recognize the illusion,
The mind works hard to create,
And stop it before it's too late.
It is our thoughts that create our world,
What you believe will unfold,
It has been told.

Emotional Control

As with the idea of thought control, emotional control can also appear to be a contradiction in terms; controlling something that feels so out of control when it happens. Controlling your emotions can also have negative consequences to your health. Your emotions are a form of communication, sending neuro-chemical messages to your brain and body. Emotions are not rational. But, they are as valid a form of communication as your thoughts and are of course linked to your thoughts and other unconscious learned patterns. Holding back from the expression of your emotions is therefore a refusal to acknowledge and listen to your internal communication that is there to assist you. In order to learn how to control emotions you first have to understand that their purpose is for your benefit, whether they feel good or bad to you is not important. Avoiding their expression causes you far more pain than you can imagine and becomes a significant health risk.

There are two "real" emotional states, love and fear. Fear is biologically based, in our brain, a natural "fight or flight" mechanism that triggers our physiological "stress" response to enable us to respond to something that threatens our existence. Whilst this response historically enabled us as Humans to avoid physical extinction, throughout time we have also conditioned ourselves, to adopt this fear response to our thoughts as well as to physical threats. The result is that we can experience stress as a function of our thinking, beliefs and other mental functions as easily as we can to the physical threat of a predator. This stress builds over time and may not be recognized until it manifests in some physical form, such as illness, injury, unexplained pains, depression, addictions etc. So, whilst we may not feel that we can control our emotional responses, we can learn to control our thoughts, perceive the world differently and reduce the stress we experience. Love, the second real emotion, considered the only true emotion, is who you are. You are pure love. Love is the only emotion that can be continuous. In other words, we cannot continually experience fear, but we can continually experience love, although we may have to learn how to do this.

There are of course many emotional states that we have labels for; anger, jealousy, guilt, shame, regret, apathy, pride, anxiety, frustration, grief, all of which are based in fear. This is because they are all associated, unconsciously, with us not feeling good enough. If I feel fear it is because the world is a threatening place and I am not able enough to cope and survive. Fear is obsessive, limits growth and leads to inhibition and increased stress. If I feel angry it is because I do not have the control I feel I should have; resentment that others do have control and revenge when I feel taken advantage of are resulting symptoms. If I feel grief it is because someone has taken something from me, that I was dependent on (physically or psychologically), therefore I must be unworthy. If I feel regret, it is because I have missed out on something therefore I cannot be complete. Whilst pride can move nations, it is also divisive, defensive and vulnerable because it is measured on the basis of something external to you, the absence of which results in the experience of shame. It is also strongly linked with arrogance and denial, which blocks growth and the acquisition of personal power. Guilt and shame are associated with having failed in some way and the need to be punished; the victim mentality, manipulation and punishment are symptoms of guilt.

Joy, courage, willingness, acceptance and reason are all emotional states associated with the one true emotion of love; there is no fear driving or underpinning them. They all have a positive influence on our life; our physical and psychological wellbeing. Courage is associated with trying new things and a willingness to deal with the challenges we face in life, with an appreciation that we can cope. Those with courage see life as exciting, challenging and stimulating. Willingness is associated with doing things at a higher level, success is common and growth is rapid. Those who are willing will always do well in life. Acceptance is the point at which major transformation takes place, the point at which you really do create your life, the point of personal empowerment. It is also related to the recognition that the source of your happiness lies within you. Acceptance is not a passive state (I accept and am helpless to change), on the contrary, it is a state of engagement with the life you are creating as your perception is widened and you take responsibility for your actions. There is no denial with awareness. Reason is the level of understanding complexity and abstraction, the relationships between things and an ability to conceptualise and comprehend. Love is not the type of love we would normally associate with attraction, hate, possessiveness, control and novelty, since this type of love is fragile and fluctuates with the experience (which means it is not love). The love referred to is that of an unconditional, permanent nature. Its source is internal to you and not dependent on someone or something. It emanates from the heart (the previous love referred to emanates from the mind). It has the capacity to lift others and accomplish great feats. It is pure and the essence of whom you are. Joy is the experience of each moment, the level of healing and Spiritual grace. Its impact on others is significant and it induces love and peace.

So with a vast emotional spectrum, clearly divided into two camps: fear and love, your emotional experiences can be very broad. The first step is to raise your awareness to your emotional states in any moment, observe them, and allow them to be experienced through you. They will pass. Try not to act on them or through them in the moment you feel them, instead watch with interest and know that you are not what you are feeling right now. You can be the observer of the experience, allowing it to flow through your body and seek to identify the cause of your emotional response. As you become aware of the thought processes, beliefs and mental patterns that cause you to respond with the emotion, so you can begin to change. Seek help if you feel you need support though this process, and remember who suffers the most when you are experiencing any negative emotional response (or worse still suppressing it)? You do. It is your body that has to handle the stress and your health that is at risk. Emotional control is possible (even when emotional responses are chemically induced through hormones) and you need to adopt higher levels of awareness and work with the thought processes that create the emotional responses in you. You need to accept that your emotional responses are not a threat to you, they are sending you a message and you need to deal with that. Suppression is not the answer.

Key Coaching Points:

* Let your emotions be your guide, learn to decode the message they are sending.

* All emotions pass, nothing lasts, good or bad.

* What you feel in any moment will also contain your memories from the past, so nothing is really as good or as bad is it feels right now.

* Fear is only ever going to block your success. Accept the fear and carry on regardless.

* Separate appropriate fear (for your physical survival) from your thoughts that hold you back. Respect physical danger and challenge your thoughts.

* Learn to love all that exists. When you love others, you can love yourself. What you hate in others, you hate in yourself.

* The stronger the emotion, the faster you will manifest the thought behind it.

* Put your energy into creating positive emotional experiences rather than avoiding negative ones.

* Allow your feelings to flow, you will cope.

Handling Fear

Fear plays a most dangerous game,
In our brain.
Confusion, discomfort, you will find,
In your mind.
Withdrawing, denying, avoiding and more,
Is the score.
Thinking, emotion, decision making so poor,
At your core.

Let fear out, let it go,
Take on the thing that scares you so.
No matter what happens you will be safe,
A gift to yourself you must make.
Only your pride is hurt when you lose,
There is no need to blow a fuse.
No matter what happens you will cope,
Always live with an attitude of hope.
You are stronger than you believe,
But you must be open to receive.
You need to go where you don't want to go,
The place of uncertainty and feeling low.
You need to be okay to fail,
Knowing it's challenging you to prevail.
It's necessary to be your best,
To handle fear better than the rest.
To overcome it you must be brave,
It's only you, you need to save.

Overcoming Nerves

Anxiety gets the better of me,
It makes me want to flee,
To run and hide, not take part,
The pain runs through to my heart.

But when I slow my breathing down,
And focus on the cold air, no sound,
In my head is present now,
Just my breath, mind free, I know how.

A calmness then comes over me,
I can see more clearly, it feels so free,
I know my plan and trust what I do,
Success will come, I know it's due.

The more I play the calmer I feel,
The easier it gets to close the deal,
But I have to stay humble, focussed and true,
It's too easy for me to lose to you.

Guilt & Shame, An Ugly Game

Feeling guilt and shame,
Is a crazy thing to do,
No-one deliberately fails,
Not me, or you.

Feeling guilt and shame,
Is a trick of the mind,
Wanting you to feel bad,
So cruel and unkind.

Feeling guilt and shame,
Because you know you didn't give it all,
But what you didn't know is that,
You were protecting yourself from the fall.

Feeling guilt and shame,
For not giving your best,
Is it not punishment enough,
To be worse than the rest?

Be gentle on yourself when you fail,
No need for guilt and shame,
Be strong, commit, learn and know,
Next time you won't do it the same.

Love It & Hate It

Sometimes I love what I do,
But I can hate it too.
Sometimes it feels so good to me,
But then at times I want to flee.

When I love it I feel I can cope,
When I hate it, there is no hope.
Good or bad I can handle it,
But getting it wrong I still feel like a twit.

Love or hate, it's all about me,
My thoughts and attitudes are plain to see.
If I can love it even when it's going wrong,
Then I know I will be so strong.

For there is no place for hate,
And by the time I feel it, it's all too late.
Better to stick to loving what I do,
Knowing I can cope, stay strong, come through.

Embarrassment

I feel so embarrassed when I make mistakes,
What do others think of me?
When it's done there's no action I can take,
My heart sinks and I begin to shake.

But then a voice inside my head so faint,
Reminds me of what I need to do.
I have a job and I must commit,
There's always a chance to start anew.

My focus sharpens, I feel engaged,
At one with what I am doing.
The thought of error in the past,
Performing to my best at last.

As long as I am in this mental space, there is no place,
For embarrassed thoughts and fear.
I feel so connected now,
Everything is bright and clear.

Irrational Anger

Anger, frustration, in a rage,
Illogical, irrational, is your stage.
Nothing you can do,
Will make logic come to you.

And you know it's true,
This feeling inside of you.
Knowing you are being unreasonable,
Makes the anger treasonable.

Because anger is about yourself,
Not being heard, damaging your health.
Communicate is what you must do,
Even though it's hard for you.

Your irrational thoughts will not explain,
Your deep feeling of pain,
But you must express how you feel,
Then the pain will become less real.

And you will be able to let go,
Of the anger that controls you so,
And come to understand,
Communication is in your hand.

Nothing anyone else can do,
To take your pain away from you.
Only you can rise above,
Your anger, learn to give yourself love.

You cannot bury it deep inside,
A dangerous place for it to reside.
It must come out, you must shout,
Express yourself and learn what it's all about.

Like it or not, it's in you,
Your interpretation, control is your issue,
Learn to let go of what others do,
And focus on being happy, being you.

Angry With Myself

I feel so angry,
Burning inside,
Nothing's going my way,
There's no place to hide.

I get so frustrated,
With my inadequate play,
Not achieving what I want,
Not as good as my mate, at the end of the day.

When I am so angry with what I have done,
There's no compassion or love,
I am not worthy of such stuff,
It's simple; I am just not good enough.

I expect to be perfect every time,
Even though it's not possible to do,
I feel so inadequate,
Next to you.

I must stop comparing my *Self* to others,
And measuring me by what I do,
Instead, focus on my strengths and achievements,
And accept I am Human too.

Engage fully in what I am doing,
Loving every moment I contribute,
Not expecting a specific outcome,
This would be very astute.

I must learn to love what I do,
Not just the winning feeling,
Not allow the child in me,
To throw a strop, so unappealing.

The only thing I can control is me,
I cannot control others actions,
Accept that I am good enough,
And stop engaging in these distractions.

Emotion Follows Thought

Thoughts precede form,
This is the norm,
So why do my emotions come first?
It feels to me, my emotions just appear,
No thoughts to guide or steer.

Habits are formed,
They are easily normed.
We link what we think to what happens.
And because we judge, good or bad,
Our emotions are linked to the thoughts we had.

So in order to control my emotional state,
These old habits I must work hard to break.
Stop judging what I have done as bad or good.
Think only in terms of what's factual and true,
Then it's easy to stay calm, just like you.

Feeling Down, Getting Back Up

Sometimes I feel so down,
It's hard to see the light,
The darkness that surrounds me now,
I want to run, take flight.

I want to be in a different place,
Out of this pit of despair,
I don't know how to handle this,
I wish I didn't care.

But then I get so low there's nowhere else to hide,
Suddenly, I feel a small spark inside,
The corner turned, the mountain climbed,
I am back on my own side.

With renewed vigour I go again,
Determined to reach the top,
Knowing the effort I must put in,
Nothing now will make me stop.

Anger a Destructive Energy

Anger is such a horrible state,
It fills your mind full of hate,
A red rage inside your head,
Wishing all around were dead.

There is no sense in this place,
And in your mind there is no space,
Full of pain, no *Self* control,
No trust in your *Self* or any other Soul.

It's such a powerless place to be,
Feeling numb, no way to be free,
And then as the energy subsides,
There's nowhere for you to hide.

Guilt and shame will always follow,
An angry state, so full of sorrow,
When rational mind is back in place,
You carry on, with good grace.

It doesn't have to be this way,
Anger is a game you play,
Fear of responsibility, failing to get it right,
Is the food of your plight.

So learn to accept its okay to fail,
And that not all see the world through your veil,
Worry less about control,
And take more care of developing your Soul.

Be kind to yourself and others you meet,
Respect the other, even in defeat,
Be humble in your success
And whatever your talent, you must bless.

Dreams & Goals

Dreams are big goals, usually a long way from where we are now. Goals are those things we must achieve in order to fulfil our dreams. Some people set goals some people don't. But at some point, for you to take any action, you must have a thought process to trigger your behaviour. In other words, you must 'decide' for something to materialise. Your decision to do something can be considered loosely as a goal.

Dreams can be big or small. They are unlikely to be reachable today otherwise you would already have them. Sometimes they are so far away they are only ever going to remain as dreams and this can be enough for you to feel good. For dreams to come true, however, you will have to engage in a series of tasks to progress from where you are now to where you want to be. It is always worth checking that you really do want your dream and that you are prepared to put in the effort it is going to take to get there.

Goals will have a timescale attached to them and be reviewed regularly and amended depending on your progress and direction. They will be measurable, which, technically speaking, means happiness cannot be a goal because it is an emotional state which means it comes from within you and cannot be objectively measured. Goal setting provides you with a sense of direction, somewhere to aim for. It provides you with the motivation, energy and drive to take the actions you need to achieve your goal. It gives you something to commit to, a sense of purpose in what you are doing. It provides opportunities for learning and creativity and it gives direction to your training and practice.

Setting outcomes and tasks as goals is an easy process. Outcome goals are any outcome you want and task goals are the 'how' you will achieve the outcome goals. The process is as follows.

Identify where you are now? What is your rating, ranking, or other outcome goal that is important to you? E.g. I am a 7.2, or I run 100m in 10.65 seconds, or earn £35k per year.

Where do you want to get to and by when? E.g. I want to get to a 6.1 in 12 months, or I want to get to 10.2 seconds in 6 months, or I want to be earning £60k in the next 12 months.

Now ask yourself, what do I need to do (specifically) to get to my goal? What skills; mentally, physically, tactically and technically, do I need to improve or acquire that will get me to my goal? You may need expert advice here. You will now have a list of tasks you need to do to achieve the first steps towards your goal.

Set an action plan (timescales) and work daily to achieve the tasks you identified. Keep taking action on a daily basis. Make sure that the tasks you set can be done by you and are not reliant on someone else, who if they weren't present would mean your goal was unachievable. For example a wife who sets a goal of wanting a bigger house that relies on her husband earning a bigger salary is not a smart goal, because she has no control over him.

Review where you are on your journey to your goal by going back to Step 1 and starting the process again.

When setting your goals make sure the idea of getting the goal lights your fire. If it doesn't you are unlikely to put in the effort that is going to be needed and you may wish to change your goal.

Key Coaching Points:

✳ When you set a goal you increase your chances of achieving it by 100%.

✳ If you don't know where you are going how can you know if you get there?

✳ A directionless ship may struggle to weather the storm.

✳ Before you invest any energy and take action you need to know where you are going and for what purpose you are going there.

✳ Your goal is the light at the end of the tunnel.

✳ Don't just dream a dream, make it happen.

✳ Dreams can change if you want and allow them to.

* The path you travel will never be wasted. If you change direction along the way, the route you have taken to get this far is the right path for you.

* If you have a dream and don't have the desire to act, review your dream.

Your Dream

Nothing is ever as it first seems,
When you are deep in the pain of failure,
When you care too much,
That losing hurts forever.
You must learn to set your *Self* free.

That doesn't mean there is no pain,
No caring when you fail,
But hurt should not prevail.
When you have tried your best, be content,
The journey you are on, you have been sent.

You must keep going, getting stronger,
Being persistent in your pursuit,
Your dream is there for as long as it suits,
Only you can let it go,
It's yours, to have, if you want it, you know.

Nothing is ever as it first seems,
Whether losing or winning it's part of the dream,
The nightmare, the scream,
Only you can know if you are really prepared,
To put in the work and not be scared.

So, are you ready to commit,
To do what it takes,
Take the knocks and the breaks.
The fame and the glory,
And then... walk away at the end of your story!

Keeping Your Dream Alive

Keeping your dream alive,
Requires a strength of mind,
To control the negative thoughts in your head,
That causes you to doubt and dread.

Keeping your dream alive,
Requires you to feel your passion,
Loving everything that you do,
The challenges presented to you.

Keeping your dream alive,
Requires you to accept,
The ups and downs, the ebbs and flows,
The uncertainty, the failure, the lows.

Keeping your dream alive,
Requires you to have faith,
Nothing you do is ever a waste,
Your journey, your destiny less haste.

Dreams Can Change

Feeling stuck not knowing what to do,
Worrying about the future,
What if I don't get my goal?
What will I do without my dream?

I've got no desire to do what it takes,
Fear, uncertainty, waste of time, stops me.
But what about my dream out there,
My life will be nothing without it!

But dreams can change and so they should,
As we grow our priorities are different,
It's okay to go in a new direction,
Let go of the past, take your learning with you.

Holding on to what you don't really want,
Is simply a trick of the ego, be honest,
Let it go and find a new path,
For your innate talent is with you always.

What It Takes

Why do you want to be good at what you do,
What does it get for you?
And what will you need to give up,
To achieve what you want in life?

Are you prepared to put in the time and effort,
That is needed for your dream to come true?
Are you prepared for the uncertainty that is,
And accept that success is only for the few?

Who are you to feel that you can be,
One of the best that's ever lived?
Are you ready for the rejection and failure,
Are you prepared to unconditionally give?

If you can accept all of this is true,
And passion still runs though your heart.
If you are not deterred, but excited and ready to go,
You've already got a great start.

Learning & Talent

Human beings are constant learning machines, whether we do so consciously or not it's in our blood so to speak. From the time we are born we are learning to associate our actions with the things that happen. Through these associations we form our understanding of the world and our place within it. Learning is taking place on many dimensions; schooling, work, relationships, our *Self*, the universe, factual, conceptual, and even learning how to think. It is an essential function for our survival. If, as in many cases, people are forced to learn things that are not of interest to them (such as when at school), or exposed to ridicule when seen to fail, learning can become a painful experience, but it shouldn't be that way. There is a big difference between learning facts to be remembered for an exam and learning how to think, such as learning to question, analyse, process and evaluate, relating to different perspectives and appreciating concepts. In order to develop your Spirit, you need to undertake more than factual learning and engage in the process of understanding the world in which you live and appreciating who you are and what you are about.

Within sports and life we will get to learn specific skills, some we will be good at and some we won't. If we are good at something we might be deemed to have a talent. Our talents will be numerous and not just based on our physical attributes. How we make use of our talents is the journey we take through life. From a physical perspective, the development of skills takes time and deliberate practice, which means that we need to put in effort and create some level of challenge in what we are doing in order to become an expert at it. Many people have great talent but do not put in the effort to achieve their highest potential. Particularly this is the case for athletes who have high levels of "natural" talent, such as hand eye coordination, perception and anticipation skills. It seems that the temptation to do 'just enough" to get the outcome you want is too great. After all, why put the effort in if you can get success without putting it in? The over-talented under-performer is common and such people will never achieve their highest potential. Whatever your talents are, their value is in them being developed such that you can get the best out of yourself. Complacency will only lead to dissatisfaction and regret at the end of the day. Be sure also to recognize your talents rather than put yourself down. It is too easy to get caught in the trap of feeling you have to do better to be good enough and lose sight of the fact that you already have something very special. Value it, treasure it, nurture it and express it.

Key Coaching Points:

* You cannot stop yourself from learning but you can slow the process down.

* Whatever your talents, you have a duty to yourself to express them.

* Failing to develop your talent is really failing.

* Complacency is fear, albeit cleverly disguised.

* Your biggest mistake in life is to think that you 'know it' or have 'got it' since there is no end to your journey.

* The greatest sadness in life comes from thinking that you have no talent. You do, you just have to recognise it.

* Choose to develop your talent to achieve your highest potential rather than feeling you have to be better because you are not good enough!

I Learn From It

Whatever I achieve I learn from it.
When I get it wrong I know,
I can change it for tomorrow.
When I win I am aware,
How to create success is clear.
I get such pleasure, feel in the groove,
Discovering how to improve.
I am not scared,
Of looking a fool,
If I get it wrong.
It doesn't matter what others think,
I am on the brink,
Of being the best I can be,
Then you will see.
I have learned to be a new me.

10,000 Hours To Be An Expert

Ten thousand hours is what it takes,
An expert to make.
All those hours of deliberate practice,
Many failures along the way,
Too much effort some would say.

But if you want to be the best,
This is time you must invest.
Developing your skills is not an option,
And developing your *Self* is a must,
If you are going to build deep trust.

So work hard with focussed intent,
Ten thousand hours of rubbish isn't time well spent.
Doing the right things for ten years and more,
Still with no guarantee, but faith,
That you can get there with good grace.

Skill Learning

Learning a skill can be hard to do,
What you need are appropriate cues.
When you think of the detailed move,
It's hard to get into the groove.
Instead you need to think with rhythm,
Words that capture the flow,
The holistic approach that brings it together,
Often works better than ever.
When the words you use have rhythm and form,
It's easier for the body to norm,
With feeling, shape and texture too,
You'll be amazed at what it will achieve for you.
So don't think too technically,
When you are learning something new,
Just get a feel for it,
With an image or two.

Learning With Images

The mind likes to work with symbols,
Words can be so confusing,
To process learning a physical skill,
With mind is so bemusing.

When there is lots of mental processing,
It's harder to perform,
Then when things start to go wrong,
The mind creates a storm.

Sensing, seeing, feeling, hearing,
Captures so much more,
It makes performing easier,
Because it's in our body's store.

So use symbols, metaphors and images,
To help you learn your skills,
Engage in how it feels inside,
Then repeat and repeat through drills.

Loving My Talent

On and on, there is no end,
To where my talent will take me.
The future is bright,
My talent the light,
For everyone to see.

In this place there is no space,
For time to cause me pressure.
I know I will win,
There is no sin,
In thinking I am better.

My journey is pre-destined, it's in my blood,
No one day is as it seems.
Whether I win today matters not,
Success isn't just about what I got,
It's about my talent, my light, my dreams.

Respect My Talent

To be blessed with a talent is a wonderful gift,
It's a privilege given to me.
Sometimes I forget how lucky I am,
In my obsession to be the best I can be.

I worry at not being good enough,
That my goals won't be achieved,
That it will all be a waste,
If I don't get there in haste.

I forget that I can express,
That with which I am blessed.
And if I put in the effort and time,
What I want to achieve can be mine.

It's not something that can be rushed,
The quality needs to be good.
I must be persistent over again,
Then I will get what I am due, and when.

I must respect the talent I have,
Not be selfish and stubborn for more,
Develop my skills the best I can do,
Be true to me, not compared to you.

When In Doubt, Keep Going

When you are good at what you do,
It can be hard to see through,
The thoughts and doubts that make it tough,
Have you think you are not good enough.

When you allow your talent to shine through,
Work as hard as you can do,
You deserve all that you get,
Taking on the challenge, winning the bet.

So when doubt comes to haunt your mind,
Tries to stop you, in your talent you find,
The strength to carry on and be,
The best you can for all to see.

Performing & Certainty

Performing is an art and the mindset required of a performer is very different from that needed for training. Athletes need to learn the differences between the two mindsets and train themselves to perform not just train to develop their skills. Whether you are giving a presentation, performing on stage, or competing in an event, you are a performer. There may be a crowd watching you, or you may be alone, but even if you are alone you are watching yourself. Always act as if you are performing to a crowd even if there is no-one present. This will help you to train yourself to perform.

Over thinking is one of the biggest problems for performers who analyse what they are doing as they are doing it (including presenters). Again, this analysis is driven by your fear of getting it wrong and wanting to be right, but it prevents you from executing your skills to the best of your ability, as you are actually 'stuck in your head'. When you are performing think of yourself as commanding the stage. Wherever your stage is doesn't matter, but it is your space, your territory, your show. You run it as you want. Planning to perform is critical, but performing to a script should not be attempted. If you plan well enough you should be able to be creative within your performance. In some cases that creativity will simply come through in the expression of what you are doing, such as with a musician. With an athlete that creativity may be expressed in your strategy, flexibility, responsiveness and calmness. With a presenter it may come through in the content of your presentation, your delivery style and the way in which you use your whole body to communicate to your audience. When performing, what you know and the skills you have is not where your attention needs to be. Instead you need to be 'engaged' fully in what you are doing such that you and the performance become one. The thinking is done in the planning, the analysis can wait until the end, stay aware in the moment and let go.

Certainty, the Human dilemma – well, it's one of them anyway! People strive to 'know', to have certainty in their lives. This is of course understandable. If you can predict you can work through habit; you don't have to think about everything in order to function effectively. If you couldn't predict you would have to work very hard to work out what was happening every second of your lives. But most people strive to 'know' and be 'right' to the extreme; to a level that holds them back from achieving their highest potential. They become fearful if they do not know, feel pressure if they cannot guarantee their outcomes, feel incompetent if they get it wrong. Yet uncertainty is what really makes us tick. When you really look at it, it is uncertainty that causes us to strive to find out, creates the challenge in our lives and leads us to feel competent as we overcome these challenges. If you knew everything that would happen every day, if you knew the result of every game you played before you played it, how much pleasure would there be in life? Even if your results were in your favour, what pleasure would there be in performing? It may be okay the first couple of times around, but you would soon lack stimulation and find the whole thing rather tedious. The key, as with most things in life, is striking the balance; enough certainty to feel safe and enough uncertainty to feel challenged. Remember, the more challenged you feel and the more you overcome, the more you will achieve in life. The more able you are to handle and even embrace uncertainty the less fear you will experience and the greater your chances of achieving your highest potential. And, until you take it on, you will never know!

Key Coaching Points:

✳ When performing it is not a rehearsal, make it happen.

✳ Performing is a no-thinking state, with awareness and a faith in your *Self*.

✳ To share with others is the gift you have as a performer.

✳ It's not the errors you make it's how you recover from them that matters.

✳ Expecting to be perfect is the root of failure, striving for it in training and letting go to perform is the key to success.

* Critical analysis is the antithesis of performance.

* Performance requires trust, without it you are dead in the water.

* The only thing that is certain in life is uncertainty.

* If everything was known there would be no fun in life. If everything was unknown there would be no stability in life.

* You have to feel some discomfort every day if you are going to grow.

* The world is moving in one direction, if you stop growing you are going backwards.

* Uncertainty brings challenge, challenge brings opportunity and opportunity brings transformation.

* Handling uncertainty is simply about trusting that no matter what happens you will cope... and you will.

* You are far more resilient and competent than you think you are.

* Uncertainty is for a life of adventure, certainty is for a life of boredom.

* "Maybe" is the only word you need to master!

It's About You

You are the star of the show, you know,
When you perform it's all about you.
Others watching, or maybe not,
Your *Self* you develop throughout the plot.

When you perform you develop who you are,
You grow in order to develop the star.
It's part of the journey, whether you see it or not,
Your *Self* is really all you've got.

When you perform you are entertaining all around,
Testing your skills, your stealth, well trained.
Judging, criticized, applauded for your fame,
You are entertaining your *Self*, all the same.

You love it, that's why you perform in flow,
The challenge, the satisfaction, the pain to grow.
It's about you and always will be,
Keep loving what you do and you will see.

Performance State

The performance state is easy to achieve,
You just have to let go of all you believe,
It's like acting on the stage,
Giving a show, for the dough,
If you are good enough you are all the rage.

To perform you must let go,
Of perfectionist tendencies that will haunt you so,
Unlike acting there's no second take,
No chance for a second break,
It's not about getting it right, it's as it is on the night.

To perform you must accept what will be,
Plan, prepare, be ready, you will see,
Trust your *Self*, get out of your way.
Allow your *Self* to perform and know,
You'll go down a storm, it's your show.

Performing To Give

I feel so lucky I have something to share,
When I perform, people begin to stare,
The skills I perform are on display,
For anyone who wants to enjoy, here today.

I have such a gift to give to you, so,
The pleasure of watching my art in flow,
To impact others lives in this way,
Is such an honour I have to say.

I work so hard to be my best,
So I can share with the rest,
The delight I see,
Feeds me.

Knowing that my reasons to train,
Are to see the joy on your face again,
Through your pleasure I achieve my goal
Through my gift, I develop my Soul.

Being Human

It's difficult being Human,
Out on your own when performing,
Feeling vulnerable, it's tough,
Easy to feel not good enough.

But when you come to your senses and see,
Everyone else is just like me,
They may handle it more or less,
But they're just the same, they feel the stress.

So just relax, it's a Human dilemma,
To want to feel better than the other.
Be reassured your quest is the same,
To be the best at your game.

So be okay with being Human,
The feelings you get are very common,
Simply continue to do your best,
And let the others worry about the rest.

Pressure

I have such a good team supporting me,
I have everything I need to succeed,
I cannot let them down,
I feel the pressure all around.

What if I don't make it good,
All that wasted time that should,
Have been given to someone better than I,
Someone who could fly.

But if I give the best I can,
There's nothing more to give,
I can be happy with my lot all that I got,
And with the life I live.

Certainty

You cannot know with 100% certainty,
What the result will be.
It isn't possible to be that clear,
Which causes fear.
Unless you learn to let go of your need to know,
You cannot grow.
Into the person you want to be,
Because you will never be free,
Of fear.

No Way I Can Know

There is no way I can know,
How this performance will go.
I only need to feel so sure,
Because deep down I feel insecure.

If I can have trust and faith,
That I'll do my best to perform great,
Then I can let go of my fear,
And that will keep my head clear.

If I just do what I know works well,
I can let go of this mental hell.
Feel secure that I will do my best, and,
Let the universe take care of the rest.

Is This Right For Me?

How do I know this is right for me,
What if I'm not good enough?
I cannot cope with not succeeding,
The pain I will feel, my heart bleeding.

What if this isn't right for me,
How much time will I have wasted?
Striving for something I cannot achieve,
The pain in my heart would never leave.

Yet how can it be the wrong thing to do.
When I feel so passionate and excited?
I love the challenge and the buzz,
It's my mind that's making all the fuss.

I know there can be no guarantees,
All I can do is give it a go,
And measure success in a different way,
The right thing to do is continue, and say,

I tried the best that I could,
I gave it my all as I promised I would,
I am so proud of how far I have come,
And whatever I achieve, my journey has been fun.

Courage

Courage is a quality of a Spiritual nature. Unlike pride which is essentially based in fear, courage is considered to be based in love. It is a quality, or value, that has a higher vibrational frequency than pride and other negative emotions, which means it is beneficial to us, psychologically, emotionally and physically. Courage can be considered an antidote to fear. There is a quality of strength and calmness about courage that makes it an ideal quality for an athlete to embrace. Courageous people achieve great things and often contribute to the greater good too. I am sure you can think of many courageous acts that have happened in your lifetime. Courage extends beyond the individual because we are all inspired by acts of courage, whilst also being humbled by them. The development of courage should be one of your aspirations in life, contributing to the development of your *Spiritual Self*. With courage you can conquer whatever you set out to achieve, overcome setbacks and reach your highest potential. We have all, at some point in time, acted in a courageous manner, which means it is possible for us to be courageous on a more regular basis.

Key Coaching Points:

✳   Take on that which you fear most.

* Courage is about overcoming fear, not avoiding fear.

* Decide to be courageous and it will be easier.

* Don't let fear stop your courage coming through.

* Take the bull by the horns and ride the storm.

* If you have a passion and want to achieve something and you fear doing it, just go for it.

Lion & Mouse

The lion is so strong and proud,
His courage is easy to see.
When he roars, he roars out loud,
Just like the lion in me.

The mouse is very quiet and scared,
He is frightened and runs away.
When he squeaks he is hardly heard,
There is no mouse in me today.

Today I will be strong and brave,
And determined to do my best.
Today no energy will I save,
When I finish I can rest.

I am going to give everything,
No matter whether I win or lose.
One hundred percent I am going to bring,
Because this is something I can choose.

Strong and brave I will always be,
Giving all that I can in every way,
And everyone will easily see,
That I am doing my best today.

Many Brave Things

There are many brave things that you could do,
In your life, if you choose.
Or you can bow down to fear,
Let options pass and dreams disappear.

Many reasons you can find,
In your mind.
For not doing the things you could do,
To be a happier you.

Being brave is taking life on,
Feeling the fear and remaining strong.
Determined to overcome your plight,
Having the faith it will be alright.

When things don't go as you planned,
And you feel too weak to make a stand.
Something inside drives you beyond,
The pain, the despair, to respond.

When courage becomes your driving force,
There's no excuses, no remorse,
Options taken, choices made,
Fear quashed, the game of your life, is played.

Building Courage

It's the little things that you do,
That builds courage inside of you.
The things you take on that you would avoid,
Make the difference, drive you on,
Help you believe you are someone.

It's the feeling that you can cope,
That builds courage and instils hope.
Embracing change willing and open,
To expand your horizons, grow inside,
No thoughts of running, no need to hide.

It's the feeling of faith in your *Self*,
That builds courage, creates good health.
Loving the challenges, that is your life,
Taking on all that comes your way, no scare,
Nothing to stop you with courage your prayer.

Tiger & Lion

The lion said to the tiger, "shall we play today to win?"
The tiger replied "of course".
They set off in battle,
But tiger threw his rattle,
When lion beat him with a pass.
Tiger came at him again,
And created some pain, but in vain.
Lion was strong and calm,
He didn't let tiger in.
And it was clear to see,
That tiger was under pressure.
He was looking flustered and in a panic,
And trying too hard to win.
But lion was cool and sticking to his plan,
Confident and courageous too.
Anyone watching would know the score,
Tiger was almost out of the door.
Lion had clearly won the day,
Staying calm and focussed all the way.

Courage

A courageous performer is who you are,
When you overcome problems you are a star.
Don't give in,
It would be a sin.

A courageous act is standing tall,
When you feel about to fall.
Keep up the fight.
You will be alright.

A courageous thought you can perform,
When overcoming fears becomes your norm.
You are on the way.
No delay.

A courageous life is one worth living,
Lots achieved and lots you've given.
You've come far.
You are a star.

Courage Is Very Real

Courage is a positive state,
In each of us to feel,
Whether or not inspired by pain,
Courage is very real.

Courage feels great,
It's deep and free,
No threat experienced,
Inside of me.

Courage feels strong,
It's solid yet calm,
No doubts or worries,
No fear of harm.

Courage feels expansive,
It's all around,
My heart, my Soul,
On solid ground.

Courage feels invincible,
Like a protective shield,
A guiding energy
Your *Self* revealed.

Have Courage

Have the courage to love,
The courage to give,
The courage to choose,
And the courage to live.

Have the courage to receive,
The courage to say no,
The courage to express,
And the courage to let go.

Have the courage to feel pain,
The courage to feel joy,
The courage to build,
And the courage to destroy.

Have the courage to be honest,
The courage to grow old,
The courage of a new born,
And the courage of your Soul.

Success & Failure

Many people believe they have a fear of failure, some think they have a fear of success. We learn very early in our lives that if we get things wrong we get punished and we feel pain, a pain that we subsequently spend the rest of our lives trying to avoid. Sometimes that is a physical pain, sometimes psychological or emotional. When young children get things wrong they can experience being ridiculed by other children, which is extremely painful. Examinations are a part of the young person's life now, they are constantly being tested and in being tested, whether a red cross appears on their work or not, they are either succeeding or failing. No amount of changing the way in which results are presented will make a difference to the fact that we all make a judgment about whether we have been successful or not. In some instances, it doesn't even matter what the official result is, we will determine in our own minds whether it was a success or not.

Of course there is no better environment that highlights this behaviour than the sports field. I have come across very few players who come off after competing saying that they did well (exceptions would be professionals who face the media after they have performed, but what they say for the press is not always what they feel). Most commonly athletes will refer to all that didn't go well and then, maybe, they will talk of how they were successful. Very often success is determined only by winning, which means there are a lot of athletes who lose and therefore fail, regularly. It is therefore important for athletes to develop measures of success that go beyond winning. If the only way you are being successful in life is to get the outcomes you want you may find yourself feeling a failure more often than not. Again, your perspective will influence your measures of success. The earlier we learn to measure ourselves in a way that reinforces our achievements, no matter how small, the greater the chance of us achieving our highest potential. The key ways in which we sabotage our success are: evaluate ourselves inappropriately, not take account of our greatness, constantly beat ourselves up for not doing as well as we would have liked, avoid pain, avoid failure, compare ourselves to others, feel inadequate, strive for perfection, and feel that we are not doing enough. When you change your perspective and the way in which you measure success, you will begin to allow yourself to achieve your highest potential.

Key Coaching Points:

✳ Success doesn't make failure any easier to take it just makes it more likely to happen!

✳ There's no such thing as failure, only feedback.

✳ You cannot have success without failure.

✳ Fear of failure or success is simply a way of keeping you safe, in your comfort zone where nothing changes.

✳ You never fail, you just run out of time.

✳ You only fail to succeed when you fear failure or success.

✳ Be gracious in defeat and humble in victory.

Focus On Your Success

Thoughts in my head,
Even before I start,
It's like a demon sitting on my shoulder,
Worries, concerns, failure and loss,
How can I be so crazy?
I tell myself all will be well.
I tell myself it doesn't matter.
I tell myself I will do my best,
I try to override this voice inside my head.
But deep down it's done its poison.

I must learn to value all that I have done.
Even when it doesn't meet my standards.
Recognise how hard I have worked,
That I deserve,
The rewards for my efforts.
I really need to back myself,
And know that I will compete,
Right till the end, I will survive,
NO defeat, only effort and pride.
NO giving up, even if it's not going my way,
Proud and strong, having fun today.
And no matter which way it goes,
Know that my success shows,
When I come through,
It's true.

Hating Losing

To hate losing is mentally weak,
No solution will you seek.
Panic will take hold too quick,
Feeling angry, dizzy and sick.

Do the thing that's mentally strong,
Accepting you might get it wrong.
You might lose even if you try,
But it's okay to feel sad and cry.

Being mentally strong is to keep on,
Never give up, when others are gone.
Look for the solution, play the game,
Rather than continue to just do the same.

Being strong is taking control,
Of your *Self* and your Soul.
Your challenge is a personal one,
Your dream, your life, your inner sun.

Spirit of Success

The Spirit of success is in your Soul,
It's part of being Human.
But the measures of success in your mind,
Are simply an illusion.
Winning creates a great feeling of achievement,
But it's not what it seems.
When losing creates such a negative response,
Your mind begins to doubt your dreams.
The true success lies inside of you,
It's about more than what you do.
It's in the expression of your talent,
So no matter what you achieve,
It's what you give that really matters.

Big Fish, Little Fish

A big fish in a little pond,
Feels great to me.
I am doing better than all the rest,
My results are easy to see.

A little fish in a big pond,
Feels lost and afraid.
Success feels so far away,
It's not easy to be brave.

But the big fish doesn't change,
Just dominates the small fish with nowhere to go.
The little fish in the big pond has room to grow,
Others to model and follow.

Success only comes to those who push,
Outside the comfort of their pond.
Only in loving to feel the discomfort
Is the place that success will be found.

Sticking To The Plan

When the challenge gets tough,
It's time to trust,
That you've prepared as well as you can.
Then just let go,
Get in the flow,
Perform and stick to your plan.

Engage in what you need to do,
It's up to you,
To get the best result you can.
You will get what you deserve,
Remember, when you perform you serve,
Without blame or fault, your fans.

A Tough Challenge

Why is it so tough to play against my friend?

I'm better than she, so it should be easy for me.
Even though I want to win, beating her feels like a sin.
It's not fair, we're friends, it shouldn't be that way,
But this is business and I must wear a mask and play.
I must play the sport, not let myself down,
I need to stay focussed on the job in hand.
Not worry about her or her feelings at all,
It's sport, it's life, we'll both come through the fall.
And friends will be friends no matter what we do,
But right now it's about me, it's not about you.

Preparing For Success

Sport is insecure and there is only one cure.
Planning, preparing and training to feel secure.

You need to feel secure, to be free to perform,
Make planning, preparing and training your norm.
Then allow yourself to be free to play,
The best you can on the day.
Create security in the ways that you can,
Accept the uncertainty, make success your plan.

Plan to Succeed

When you know what you are doing,
It's so very comforting.
When you don't know what to do, haven't got a clue,
You'll get what's coming to you.

When you know you will cope, no matter what,
It's relaxing.
You can let go of worries, there is no stress,
You are free to do your best.

When you hide, leave things to chance,
Panic, fear, anxiety your friend.
You cannot think or respond that well,
You feel you are in a living hell.

When you feel calm and secure,
In tune with the game, no fear,
Anticipation an asset for sure,
The dance of success you will endure.

You must choose to plan to win,
Know exactly what you will do.
Prepare for anything that may go wrong,
So under pressure you can stay strong.

Planning cannot guarantee success,
But, without it failure is easy to do.
Don't let fear and panic take control,
Make planning an important goal.

Safety Breeds Success

Stability is something we all need,
From this place we can succeed.
Develop our skills and talent strong,
With safety and security we feel we belong.

Creative acts can be performed,
From a safety net, created norms,
Freedom to express your gift at last,
With a strong supporting cast.

Routines and rituals keep you safe and sound,
Keep your feet firmly on the ground,
Play without them you will feel the stress,
Your nerves and panic you will have to address.

Doing the same thing over again,
Helps you feel it's all the same,
Then when things begin to go wrong,
You can still feel safe, and strong.

Success Needs Action

Success may come to those who wait,
But action you must always take,
Effort is needed every day,
No escape, it's the only way.

No matter how talented you know you are,
There's no easy way to be a star,
On this journey to the top of your game,
You must be special, not the same.

You have to work so hard it's true,
If you really want success to come to you,
Or you can sit dreaming of that time afar,
Remain in the illusion, that you are more than you are.

Pride & Contribution

Pride is a fascinating quality of experience to talk about, especially as someone who spent 12 years in the British Army. An Army is built on pride; it is one of the qualities that enable people to work so effectively. Pride draws people together to the extent that they would give their lives for each other. Family environments can also be very strongly bound through pride, sporting teams certainly are. Pride, in the sense of feeling a sense of achievement with what you have done is generally considered a worthy quality. We feel good about ourselves if we can say we are "proud" of what we have achieved. But there are also less helpful aspects to pride. They are qualities of stubbornness and proving that can result in harm to oneself and even others, a refusal to budge on something which can keep you stuck doing what you have always done. The term 'pride before a fall' reflects this aspect.

Pride can be a quality of experience that is based out of fear; the fear that we are not good enough. When we feel pride, we feel we have overcome something therefore the underlying feeling is one of being less than, or inadequate. For example, we like to have pride in our appearance, possibly because we want others to judge us well, or we judge poor dress as being a reflection of something negative, or again, perhaps because it simply helps us feel good about ourselves. Either way, pride is based on a value (good or bad) judgment, which is at odds with our *Spiritual Self*, which says that we are always good enough. In other words, there is always more to us than our visual appearance, more to us than what we say and do, and more to us than what we achieve. We just have to learn to tap into that source of being good enough, that is to say, develop our *Spiritual Self* and some aspects of pride can prevent this. However, that said, most people can relate to pride in its positive sense and feeling proud can be a great source of inspiration, especially in sport and tribally based environments. Pride also drives people to take action and support each other.

Contribution is about what you put into what you are doing. Most people when thinking of their contribution measure themselves on their physical effort, because it is the most familiar measure of contribution. Rarely do people consider the mental and emotional, effort that they are putting into what they do. It is probably not that natural to you to first look at whether you are in a positive emotional and mental state before evaluating your physical effort. This is an error in evaluation, because your physical behaviours emanate as a function of your emotional state and thought processes. So to assess your contribution to what you are doing, begin to look at the attitude with which you are doing it, look to your emotional state, and only if this is appropriate look to your physical contribution. There is a saying in business, 'don't change your marketing strategy change your energy'. That is what I am saying to you. You cannot possibly assess your true contribution unless you consider your emotional and mental contribution. When you change your emotional and mental state you will change your outcomes.

Key Coaching Points:

* Do only those things that you will feel proud of.

* Be at least as proud of what you put in as you are of what you get out.

* Don't allow stubbornness to get in the way of common sense.

* Give and you shall receive.

* It's what you put in that counts, not what you get out.

* The only true value is the value of your effort, everything else results from that. If you don't like what you are getting out, you need to change what you put in!

Tears In My Eyes

I've got tears in my eyes,
I tried so hard, I couldn't have tried any harder.

I've got tears in my eyes,
I focussed so well, I couldn't have been more focussed.

I've got tears in my eyes,
I gave so much, I couldn't have given any more.

I've got tears in my eyes,
Even though I lost, I couldn't have been any braver.

I've got tears in my eyes,
I'm so proud of myself, I couldn't feel any prouder.

Passion or Proving?

When passion is strong the heart is free,
Fear does not get in the way.
When your mind is engaged in proving your worth,
Passion is lost and the pain gets worse.

Never giving up is a quality admired,
But when driven by the mind, one gets bound by pride,
Having passion and drive from the heart's fire,
Keeps you going with joy, love and desire.

When proving you are someone or something,
Is what you feel makes your heart sing,
It's only your *Self* you will deceive,
As you are only as good as what you achieve.

Keep your passion strong with an open heart,
Stay in love with what you do, and be true,
Don't be dragged into the illusion of fame,
Accept the pain, with nothing to lose and all to gain.

Pride Your Demise

Feeling stuck,
Stubborn and proud,
Not hearing the messages,
Coming to you so loud.

Don't ask for help,
Don't admit you're wrong,
High opinion of yourself,
Your only song.

Need for status,
Pride your demise,
Fear your demon,
No-one to hear your cries.

Pride a Virtue

A sense of achievement,
Feeling so proud,
Recognition for your efforts,
Coming to you so loud,

Team Spirit,
Personal success,
Giving to others,
You are blessed.

Satisfaction and pleasure,
Pride a virtue in you,
Love your grace,
You are being true.

Being Smart

Just be brave and be strong,
And trust the result will come along.
Stay focussed, and work hard,
And tactically play the smart card.
When you do these things with love,
You'll get the result you're capable of.
You can be proud giving your best in this way,
It's not about what others say.
You did all that you can do,
No-one can ask any more of you.
So always put in 100%, and,
No matter the result, be happy and content.

Your Contribution That Counts

Take pride in what you do,
Then you will feel good, about you,
It's what you put in that makes a difference,
Not what you get out, that's cheap and insignificant.

As you perform, love the feeling,
Of knowing how much you are giving,
Developing yourself, developing your Soul,
A stronger, healthier person your goal.

Whether you win, or whether you lose,
When you're engaged in the process, you choose.
Don't fear the pain of not achieving,
It's far less than the pain of regret and grieving.

When you don't put in effort, when you give up,
You will always feel not good enough,
And regret the opportunity not taken,
Your destiny in the making.

When you contribute all that you can,
Work hard to give of yourself,
Because you will have given your best,
You can only ever feel a success.

Take pride in what you do,
And always feel good about you,
Trust that what you put in, you will get out,
But remember, it's your contribution that counts.

Pride, Grace & Vice

When pride is your grace,
It's not about saving face.
It gives you personal satisfaction,
Encourages you to take action.
Supporting others in their dreams,
Connect all to the universal stream.

When pride is your vice,
Your attitude is not very nice.
Arrogance your stance,
Stubbornness your trance.
Elevate yourself through social status,
Separation from the source that connects us.

Confidence & Belief

One of the most common concerns, feelings, thoughts, among the Human species is the idea that they "lack confidence". The concept of confidence is an interesting one and needs to be broken down into something more tangible to be understood. Such a generalized comment as "I lack confidence" is the most debilitating thought that you can have. The idea that you lack confidence can only limit your development. I use the term 'idea' deliberately, because confidence is essentially a feeling you have based on judgments you have made and is therefore a construction of the mind and an illusion. The thought processes that lead people to feel a lack of confidence are based around not being good enough, and therefore based in fear. Your standard of performance is as it is in any moment and if you are training you should be confident that you are constantly improving. You can always feel confident in your ability as it is now, but you cannot expect perfection or build your confidence on the basis of 100% success and guarantees. You do not know if you will win, but worrying that you might not will only lead to under-performance. Clearly, for most people, the higher their level of skill the more confident they feel about undertaking the task. However, this thought pattern is based on the fact that, with higher skills you have a greater chance of success and therefore less chance of failure. Since failure is something you want to avoid, failure is an underlying measure linked to a lack of confidence. Instead of this insane cycle, start to think in terms of feeling confident that you will do your best (no matter what the outcome). Be confident that you are improving all the time. Be confident in your ability to learn and don't expect that you should know or be good at everything you do. Be confident that no matter what happens you will cope with it. Be confident in yourself, recognizing you are good enough. Be confident that you will never give up, you will push to the end and you will come through. Be confident that you have prepared well. Success reinforces confidence, it doesn't provide the foundations! You also need to recognize that a little anxiety is a sign that you are pushing outside of your comfort zone, so you can be confident that this feeling is a sign that you are growing; embrace it.

What you believe will come true for you. You live your life in accordance with your beliefs. But ask yourself, how did you come to follow the beliefs that you do? Were they given to you by your parents and others, society and cultural norms? Do you have evidence for your beliefs and if so what? Is that evidence based in the past or present moment? If it is the past, is it still true or are you maintaining its truth through your behaviour? Many things that were factually correct in the past are no longer true, so even scientifically proven facts may not be correct. If you are old enough or have studied history you will remember that at some point in time, the world was proven to be flat and if we went to the end of it we would fall off! It was scientifically proven that the Human body could not withstand the pressure of running a 4 minute mile! Also, it was thought to be true that the sun moved around the earth. Facts are changing all the time with new knowledge and understanding of how things work. You need to reinvent yourself by challenging the beliefs you hold. It is not so important to ask whether they are true or not as it is to ask "does this belief help me achieve what I want?" If what you believe is not supporting you, give yourself permission to change it.

Key Coaching Points:

* Do not live through your history, do what is right for you.

* Confidence comes with trust and faith in your *Self*.

* When you believe you need no evidence, when you don't believe no evidence will suffice.

* There is no such thing as over confidence, but what does exist is complacency.

* Be true to yourself to develop your confidence.

* Stick your stake in the ground, what you like and want, and care less about what others think about your choices.

* Skills you may have more or less of, but your faith in yourself is infinite, you just have to learn that you are okay just the way you are!

* In striving to be better, you run the risk of feeling that you are not good enough.

* Be confident in those things you can control and measure yourself less on the outcomes you didn't achieve!

* What you believe, whether positive or negative, you can achieve.

* Where your energy flows your attention goes.

* Believe what works for you, not what holds you back, no matter how true others may think it is.

Never Good Enough

Sometimes I feel it's never enough,
No matter what I do.
There's always more,
I should do better,
Never satisfied even if I tried.
The journey is rough,
Never being good enough!

But that's the challenge,
That keeps us going,
To improve on what we've done,
It's not personal to anyone.
There's more to you than what you do,
You need to become *Self* aware,
And start to care.

So feel free to challenge yourself,
There's always more to be done.
But know you are always doing your best,
Even when you do much less,
Than you feel capable of.
Enjoy the journey when it's rough,
And know that you are always good enough.

You can know this is the game,
A trick the mind likes to play.
It keeps you striving, keeps you moving,
Results in your success along the way.
But you are more, much more than this.
What you achieve is not who you are,
Whatever you do, you are already a star.

Recovered My Faith in Me

When I lose my belief,
I feel weak, vulnerable, unsafe.
Fear is strong and doubt is high,
I know I will fail, no way,
To save the day.
My mind telling me why,
I can't succeed,
But I must bleed,
Myself dry,
I must try,
Know that I am safe,
Inside myself I have my faith.
Stronger than belief,
Is my faith in me.
Because, when the day is done,
No matter what's gone on,
I am still someone.

Confidence is Earned

Confidence based only on success,
Is short lived and vulnerable.
Threatened by the ebb and flow,
Of how all performances go.

Confidence must come from something,
You can control and change in you, like,
Knowing you have put the hours in,
There's no quick route if you want to win.

Confidence must come from belief,
In your *Self* and what you do.
It's not about guarantees of success,
It's about learning to handle the stress.

Confidence comes from letting go,
Of the illusion of power,
You get from beating others,
Because, then it's only you that suffers.

Feeling confident when your performance is poor,
Can only happen if you have faith,
That you have done all that you can for sure,
And whatever will be, will be; this is law.

Confidence must come before results,
You have to "act as if".
Of course it feels good when success you make,
But that's the icing on the cake.

Confidence is in you, it's about sticking to your plan,
Having skills and developing them the best you can.
Accepting that you can't always win,
And if you don't it isn't a sin.

You can always be confident in what you do,
No matter what results you get for you.
Have faith you will achieve your dreams,
Feeling confident is not as difficult as it seems!

Being Honest With Your Self

Be honest with your *Self*,
You know *You* too well,
To cheat yourself into thinking,
You are better, it's a spell.

Don't try and hide,
Your weakness and pain,
Be honest with yourself,
Then you can change your game.

There's nothing wrong with making mistakes,
It's how we learn and grow,
You cannot stop the negative,
Your energy must flow.

Hiding blocks success, so,
You cannot achieve your potential,
Being honest with your *Self*,
For self-esteem is essential.

Being true to your *Self,*
Builds your Soul and leaves you free,
Achieving, learning, growing,
To be the best that you can be.

Believe Is Not Needing To See

If you have to experience to believe,
You will never have faith.
If you need to win to believe,
You will never have confidence.

Faith comes without evidence,
Confidence too,
And what you believe, changes you.
To be a success in what you do,
You need to believe what helps you,
Not what your mind thinks is true!

Time

Time is a mental construct. We have clock time, which we cannot change and we have perceptual time, which changes as a function of our thinking and emotional state. We can make time feel endless or we can make it feel as if there is not enough. In all cases, time is a construction of the Mind and not of the *Spiritual Self*, which is without time and space; endless and infinite. Your thought processes and your ability to manage your emotional state is therefore important in how you perceive time. Those who are always feeling that time is running out and there is never enough time will have a very different interpretation and perception of the world as compared with those people for whom time is plentiful. And yet, we all live in the same world with our clocks ticking at the same pace. We often hear people talk about the pace of life speeding up, and it certainly feels that way. Transmitting phone signals, television and other electronic communication happens in an instant, where previously it would have taken weeks, months, and even years to communicate across the planet.

However, it is us, Human beings that determine how fast things are actually moving, and we do this inside our heads. People who object to this way of thinking refer to deadlines that they have to meet, usually imposed on them and in this respect there can be occasions when there is more work to do than there is time to do it. But in the majority of cases time is rarely the real issue, motivation is the issue and an inability to prioritise effectively.

Personal development is becoming a victim of the "time" mentality. We are all striving to get there more quickly than before and there is pressure on younger and younger people to get to specific standards before a certain age or they will be considered to have failed. This is of course one of the practical realities of competing at the highest level in sport; to be better than others, and is also true within education and business. But you also have to find some way to control your perception of time so as to not feel inappropriately stressed.

However, if you are living life under the constant threat of time, you are missing the point. The only true time is now. Tomorrow doesn't exist, there is just "now". Whatever is happening, it is happening now. Even the thoughts in your head are happening now. If you are thinking about the past or the future you are making it real to you now, because the thoughts in your mind are having an effect in your body right now. The important point then becomes, think about only those things that support you now!

Key Coaching Points:

✳ Your body has to be in the now, your Mind needs to align with your body.

* It's easy to live in the past we are doing it all the time; that's called *Habit*.

* To live in the now requires awareness.

* If we dream of the future we can make it come true for us, if we dream of the past we can make it come true for us...dream only of what you want.

* Whatever happens, for good or bad, it will pass.

* Change requires that I am aware of my habits and choose not to follow them.

* Your investment of time in anything you do is never wasted, but that doesn't mean it is right to continue doing it!

Time On My Side

Time waits for no-one,
But it can be fun.
Sometimes it goes so fast,
And everything is such a blast.
And then it goes so slowly I feel free,
Time feels so good to me.

And then time can go so fast,
The panic seems to last,
Feeling alone, lost and cold,
I have nothing on which to hold.
No matter how I try to feel free,
Time is now my enemy.

If only I could make time stand still,
Have all the time, maintain the thrill.
Correct what has gone before,
Even the score.
When I let go of my pride,
Time will be on my side.

There is only one true time,
It's the present and it's not mine.
I need to let go of the future and the past,
Recognise that nothing can last.
Control my mind through my thought,
Then by time I can never be caught.

Tomorrow Never Comes

My fear is so strong that I will get it wrong,
And what if I invest so much time?
What a waste,
Less haste,
I can always change tomorrow,
No sorrow.

But tomorrow comes and it's always the same,
My fear doesn't go away.
No way out,
Only doubt,
I will never change tomorrow,
I feel such sorrow.

There is only one way to overcome this state,
To break through this barrier to my success.
Go for it now and say it out loud,
Be strong and proud,
For tomorrow never comes,
Today is my only sun.

Time Is Against You

Time is such a curious thing,
When it's on your side, it makes your heart sing.
But when things aren't going great,
Time is against you, it's all too late.

Setting time can help your goals come true,
In this way it focuses you.
But when you fail to achieve what you said,
Time is a burden; it gets into your head.

Never enough time to do all you will,
Time can be a bitter pill.
The cause of stress when there's not enough,
Time can make it feel so tough.

But when you take one step after another,
Time doesn't have to be a bother.
Only when you're in a rush to the top,
Will time become the cause of your flop.

Time To Quit

When the sun goes down,
Dark all around,
And you know it's time to quit,
You sit,
And wonder with awe,
You've achieved more,
Than you ever thought you might,
So right,
For you to follow the path you did,
The blood, the tears, the good and the bad,
You had,
It all along the way,
There's nothing more for you to say,
Except,
Goodbye, it's been a blast,
Right up to the very last,
And now my time has passed.

W.I.N.

Present time is so easy to do,
It's a discipline of attention.
By focusing on, **W**hat's **I**mportant **N**ow,
There will be fewer distractions.

Allowing the mind to wander to future or past,
Sucked into external trivia and farce.
Critical of your *Self*, thinking you have to do so much,
Too late, the time has passed.

Present time is easy to do,
When you value it enough to take action.
Focus on, **W**hat's **I**mportant **N**ow,
There will be fewer distractions.

Loss of Heart & A Fixed Mind

If you set your mind to it you can do anything,
There's always enough time.
Energy unbounded, feeling fine,
In your mind you can achieve
All you desire, all that you believe.

But when you expect with date and time,
You have a fixed idea, a deadline,
There's never enough time, energy is hard to find.
And if you are distracted by what you missed out on,
Any chance of success is gone.

A loss of heart comes with a fixed mind,
Passion wanes and doubt creeps in,
Missing that deadline feels such a sin.
But your highest potential is there for you,
When you are focussed on what you need to do.

The Power of Hope

Sometimes it feels so hopeless,
There's nothing I can do,
Time moves too quickly,
And I don't know how to pull through.

I feel so helpless I want to give up,
Escape, run away, throw the towel in,
But then when all hope is gone I relax a bit,
A glimmer of light, I see a way that I could win.

A sense of hope comes over me,
A feeling deep inside,
And I am connected with my dream,
I'm not going to let it slide.

No way back,
To that hopeless place,
I'm here now, in the flow,
And time is moving so slow.

My senses restored,
My thinking clear,
No more fear, and success is near,
I am here.

Choices & The Review

It is easy to think that we do not make that many choices in our lives. We are brought up by parents and significant others who guide and direct our behaviours, likes, dislikes, thoughts and feelings according to their understanding and personal experiences. We follow cultural and societal norms and rules, whether we want to or not. So it is fair to ask whether we really do have a choice or are we just pawns in the social system within which we exist? One thing that is true; whatever you believe you will make happen. So if you think you do not make choices, you won't and if you think you do you will live your life in that way. Whilst you may not be able to control what happens outside of you, you can certainly choose how you respond. With every choice there are consequences, so if you chose not to follow a social rule there would potentially be a price to pay, but this does not mean you have no choice. Every action you take, and of course those that you don't, during your life is a choice of free will.

The choices you make determine the direction your life takes. The more consistent your choices are with your *Spiritual Self*, the more content your life will be. When you compromise your *Self* and do things through obligation and loyalty with an expectation of something in return, you may find you experience pain and misery. When you feel you have no control over your life, you cannot say "no" and you take on responsibility for others, you may come to feel bitter and resentful. Recognising that you are making choices, and that you created your life as it is now, however painful that may at first feel, is the first step to becoming personally empowered. Whether that is recognizing that you choose your emotional response as you fail to get the result you wanted, or that you can choose to divorce your husband because you are no longer in love with him, you are now on the road to recovery. Yes, of course there are consequences and sometimes they may seem insurmountable. But, remember you are stronger than you think, all things pass and no matter what the future holds, if what you are currently doing isn't working for you it's time to make a new choice. It is only through our choices that we come to learn what is right for us and what is not. We learn to connect our outcomes with our choices, become aware of the significant impact we have on our lives and start to live the life we want.

Looking back at what you have achieved, or not, is something we all do from time to time and perhaps more so in later life. The mid-life crisis can be linked to this evaluation when the realization hits that there are potentially more years passed than there are left to go and you wonder what you have to show for it. This time of 'crisis' comes about as people review where they are, reflect on unfulfilled dreams and become acutely aware of the marital and family situation they now find themselves in. Sporting careers can be very short, some starting very young such as gymnastics, and the period of time and level of personal investment can be extremely intense. This means that for many athletes, their sporting career is but one fraction of their "working time" which means you have to ask the question, what next? Even those not engaged in sports careers will, in this modern world of high mobility, most likely find themselves changing jobs and even career direction on more than one occasion during their working lives. And, of course, all the aspects of our lives, including relationships, personal development, social and family etc will have start and end points throughout their evolution. Everything we experience in life follows this cycle of birth, life and death. It cannot be stopped and if you try you will experience considerable pain. So what becomes really important is that when you look back at what you have achieved you feel content, satisfied and that your time has been well spent. Anything less than that is likely to cause you to feel your life to date has been a waste. Clearly, your perception of what you have done will be influenced by your perspective, the goals you set or didn't and your expectations and thinking patterns. Be sure you give yourself the best chance to see the good that you have achieved. It's too easy to look back and think you've failed.

Key Coaching Points:

⁎ Choose the life you want and want the life you choose.

✳ Any decision you make is a choice. With all choices there are consequences.

✳ To deny your choices renders you powerless.

✳ You cannot control what happens outside of you, but you can choose how you respond to it.

✳ Whilst you function through habit your choices are limited.

✳ To recognize you have a choice you must first become aware of what you want and where you are going, otherwise you will follow the choices others make for you.

✳ When you look back focus on how far you've come rather than what you missed out on along the way.

✳ Hindsight is a wonderful thing, but don't use it against yourself!

✳ Look through the lens of your achievements not your expectations.

✳ If you are not achieving what you want, don't wait to the end to say I told you so, change something now.

✳ Remember, whatever you are doing today you will have to justify to yourself tomorrow.

✳ When it's time to stop or change, let go with grace.

Love or Fear, You Choose

Love or fear, you choose.

When you love all that you do,
There is no place for fear.
When you are losing, you love no-one,
Not even yourself so dear.

When hate comes through, there's no true love,
Just a fear that you are not good enough.
With fear in winning, you can never win,
With love in losing you can never lose,

Love or fear, you choose.

Poor Me, Love Me

Why is it so hard to see the good?
When all around tell me I should.
Oh no it's me.

If I fail it can't be right,
How can I see with new sight?
Poor me.

How can I change what I believe is true?
The evidence makes me feel so blue.
Someone save me.

But if others can see things differently,
There must be more that I can be.
Brave me.

If I take responsibility for my perception,
See things from a different direction.
I free me.

If I let go of my destructive side,
And see all the good beyond my pride,
I can love me.

Take Control of Your Responses

When I think that things happen to me,
I will never see.
When the outcome I get drives how I feel,
My weakness revealed.
When I make my results so personal,
I'm in trouble.
I am not in control you see,
Things just happen to me!

When I realize I choose how I feel,
It's real.
The outcomes I get come from what I put in,
I am strong.
I can feel good even if I haven't done my best,
That's the test.
I am in control of how I react,
That's a fact.

Deep lasting confidence is there you see,
When I take control of me.
When I learn how to observe,
My mind will serve.
When outside events control my actions,
My emotions become a distraction.
When I am powerless to perform,
Random becomes the norm.

So take control of how you react,
You cannot change what's happened, that's a fact.
But you can choose all that you do,
Rather than think it's just happening to you.
See things for what they truly are,
Events in life, not intended to scar.
Make sure you think to suit your own aim,
Stay composed, and play the game.

Looking Back

When your sport is ended,
You have done all you can,
And you look back,
What do you see?

Did you give all that you could give?
Overcome the challenges there to do,
Or did you excuse your poor performances,
Fear, blame and regret, the legacy of you?

As you look back now, of what are you proud?
Did you raise your game when it mattered,
Or do you see yourself in shame,
Giving up, giving in, easily shattered?

Make sure what you do every day,
Will ensure that you look back and say,
I gave it all that I could do,
I am proud of my achievements and my losses too!

The Review

When it feels like it's a disaster,
There's nothing you can do,
Except sit back and review.
How was your state before you performed?
Did you sleep good, eat well?
Was there anything different, as far as you can tell?
When did it start to all go wrong?
What happened, what did you think and feel?
Only you know what's really real.
And how did you respond to it?
Were you calm, focussed, trusting, unfazed,
Or did you panic, get flustered, feel in a haze?
How did you feel about turning it around?
Did you try gently to get it right or make it a fight,
Did you trust your plan, do all that you can?
And if you had the chance, would you do it all again,
What would you do differently, and what the same?
To change the outcome of the game.

When The Time Has Come

When the time has come,
The game is done.
There's nothing more you can give,
You can still live.

Walking on with head held high
Knowing you tried your best to fly.
Happy, you gave it your all,
Still standing tall.

No regrets, no wishes left undone,
Everyone's time must surely come.
It's a truth we must accept,
Now, we're past our best.

But there's always something out there for you,
Something exciting, something new,
You can always reach for the sun,
Your journey's a never ending one.

Spiritual Self

In describing Human evolution we have been through the era of cognitive intelligence, the era of emotional intelligence and we are moving into the era of the Spiritual intelligence. Your *Spiritual Self* is an aspect of you that is generally considered to be beyond your Mind and thought processes; aspects such as intuition, awareness, forgiveness, acceptance and the recognition that there is a "higher dimension" that has some influence over your life. That higher dimension is often referred to as "God", but "God" has different meanings to different people. It is not my intention to reflect a religious perspective here as I do not follow or subscribe to any religion. God, in the terms referred to in the verses below, is intended to reflect our higher connectedness, to our collective consciousness and the higher part of our *Self* that is not motivated through our Ego. Also be assured that in talking about your *Spiritual Self*, there is no intention for you to become some wacky, flower power, hippy, with a laissez faire approach to life. Your *Spiritual Self* is already a part of you, always has been and always will be. Expressing your innate Spiritual dimension is the aim of the verse included here. It is precisely because our *Spiritual Self* is an aspect of us that it is considered still within our domain of influence, which makes our choices in life even more important.

You may already be familiar with the Spiritual part of your *Self*; for example, through experiences you have had, a major and sudden shift in your priorities (perhaps away from money and towards contribution), an awareness and trust that something greater than you exists and is operating with you, prayers that have been answered, support that has been provided when you needed it, intuitions that have saved you in some way, hunches or irrational decisions that paid off, faith in something for which you had no hard evidence, a sense of knowing (without evidence) that you are doing the right thing, unexplained feelings, visions or voices giving you guidance, creative ideas that seem to come out of the blue, near death experiences and significant emotional shifts that you cannot logically explain. These experiences may have been glimpses, some you may have even ignored, or they may have been more prolonged experiences over a period of time during which you have been aware of feeling a level of joy and contentment that is unexplained within your current circumstances. The questions you ask also reveal your Spiritual dimension such as: Why am I here? What is my purpose in life? For what purpose did that happen to me? What is there here for me to learn? What can I contribute/give back to this?

It is thought that we make some significant changes at a Spiritual level during different phases in our lives. Often big shifts will happen between the ages of 29 and 31 and between 35 and 42. It is therefore no coincidence that major changes in significant relationships, careers, and living location take place during these times. There are also changes within our energy system that, according to Chinese Medicine take place every 7 years for women and 8 years for men. Maybe that's where the term '7 year itch' came from!

Developing your *Spiritual Self* is the process of your evolution that will lead you to feel content, joyful, at peace, without fear and even enlightened. It is the process by which you learn to express the pure love that you are. You operate your life through forgiveness and begin to experience higher levels of awareness. You let go of the Ego Mind and its illusions and recognize that you own nothing and so nothing can be taken away from you. You are your Spirit, nothing more, nothing less, eternal.

Key Coaching Points:

* Your Spirit is eternal, everlasting, your body is temporary.

* Don't allow what you do to mean too much to you, you are more than that.

* Not everything can be explained so don't seek the answer.

* Perfection is not your goal, transformation is.

* Your journey is to discover who you are, not to be someone.

* When Spirit is strong fear is gone.

* Your Spirit is strong you just have to be aware of it.

* Spirit is the essence of who you are, your body a vehicle and your mind the illusion.

It's Not What You Do

Be okay with feeling bad,
Knowing it will go away, and be glad,
Your feelings are simply communicating, coming through,
But remember, it isn't about you, it's what you do.

What you do is not who you are,
When you want something so much it can seem so far,
It's natural to feel bad when you fail,
But don't make it a personal tale.

Let it go and try again,
But don't just do it all the same.
What you do is what you get,
Change something, no regret.

Who you are is much more than this,
What you do can never be bliss.
What you do is fraught with pain,
Because there is always loss and gain.

Who you are is beyond this plight,
Who you are is pure light.
To feel this essence pure and true,
Be aware, look beyond the physical you.

Accepting & Forgiving

When we identify with what we do,
Failure is hard to take.
When we have only one thing that is important,
Loss is harder to handle.
When we are so proud of what we do,
Letting go is hard to achieve.

When we love and accept,
Letting go is easier to do.
When we forgive ourselves for failing,
Loss is easier to handle.
When we know there is more to us than what we do,
Failure is taken as feedback.

We learn, make changes, progress, never look back,
At missed opportunities.
Only by letting go, forgiving and accepting,
Can you be truly successful at what you do.
Anything less is living in the past,
Holding your *Self* back.

My Journey

All the effort,
All the pain,
What will I gain?
I may win,
I may lose,
How can I choose?
It's what I want,
It's part of me,
Can't you see?
I have to try,
Give it a go,
I have to know?
I have a talent,
I must express,
Nothing less.
And when I'm done,
I'll feel the best,
Then I can rest.
Happy taking part,
That's the art,
My journey's start.

Servant To The Soul

My biggest ally,
My trusted friend, that is,
My mind, should be,
The servant to my Soul.
I must not let my mind take control.
My Spirit knows what's best for me.
I need to be open, let it be free.
My ego mind will always stop me,
Being the best that I can be.

Strong Spirit, Weak Mind

My Spirit is strong,
It supports me well,
In my times of need,
It is there for me, at speed.

My ego mind is weak,
Full of fear,
The truth,
It doesn't hear.

My Spirit runs deep,
It cannot be touched,
By mental weakness,
Proving, pain and lust.

My Spirit knows what's best for me,
My mind wants to show off, for all to see.
With Spirit to guide my actions,
I can succeed; no distractions.

If I let my ego mind control,
I risk the development of my Soul,
I will be guided by fear and pain,
And live my life through loss and gain.

When I let my Spirit free,
And live my life with Spirit guiding me,
Success will come in the way that's right,
And I will live with a new sight, through my light.

More Than Pride

I know there's a place deep inside,
Where what I feel is more than pride,
A deep sense of comfort I find there,
No fight, no pressure, no desire, just bare,
Yet in this barren space and time,
I am all and all is mine,
A greater connection I cannot feel,
To all that is truly honest and real.

Loneliness

The loneliest place, the sporting ground,
Whether on your own,
Or a team around.

When you are down,
There's no-one there,
To take the pain away.

Only you, alone it's true.
In your sadness and despair,
Can stand up to be counted.

Laid out bare for all to see,
Vulnerable, broken, but really free,
Even if you don't see.

As you let go, connect and soar,
There is no lonely place any more.
In your bareness, fully exposed,
Your Spirit rises strong and bold.
Never alone,
Even on your own.
Now free to see with open eyes,
Your connection to the skies.
And know that all you have ever done,
You did for entertainment and fun,
Not to feel accepted or fit into the tribe,
Only in your loneliness can you become alive.

Balance, Karma, Retribution

I feel so angry,
For getting it wrong,
Not doing what I know I can,
Why am I so inadequate?

I feel so fantastic,
For getting it right,
I have done it so well,
Why can't I do this all the time?

Balance, fairness, Karma, retribution,
All ensure an equal solution.
What goes up, must come down,
Gravity controls us all around.
So when I'm failing or feeling low,
I know there's only one place to go.
And when I'm excited and playing my best,
I must remain humble, gracious, at rest.
And know that no matter what happens today,
It can always go the other way.
Allow things to be as they must,
In the laws of the universe, I can trust.

Your Journey Is In Your Soul

When you love what you do,
It's clear in your mind,
The present, your guide,
Your journey defined.

But when your eyes are drawn,
To the end of the road,
To get the gold,
You lose your way and a fright takes hold.

You have been sold,
To the darker side of your mind.
The past and future, your only signs,
Your route now leaves you blind.

Stay in the present enjoy the gifts it brings,
Opportunities to learn and grow.
And never doubt, what you are about,
Your journey is in your Soul.

Be Patient

Be patient young Soul,
You are in such a rush for fame.
Your journey is long with much to learn,
Yet all you see is what you want to gain.

Take time to enjoy the simple pleasure,
Of testing yourself to the limit,
Push your *Self* more than you thought you could,
Your mind, your body, your Spirit.

Your sport is a tool to play the game,
Of life, it's just the way,
Enjoy each moment that comes to you,
It's always got something to say.

No need for critical evaluation,
Trust you are doing your best,
You must take time to rest,
To pass the universal test.

Be patient young Soul,
Your success will come,
Maybe not as you expect,
But nothing less.

What you are doing now is right for you,
But who knows where it will lead,
Just enjoy the ride,
Faith on your side.

Spirit In Me

When my Spirit runs strong through me,
Everything feels so easy and free,
There's nothing I own, you can see,
Nothing "I am", or have to be.

The world is my oyster, it's all open to me,
There's no time to loiter, so much to see,
So no matter what I get from what I do,
There's more to me, and there's more to you too.

Detached observer watching down from above,
Connected to all upon the ground with love,
No fear to stop me, no loss of face,
Just enjoying the journey, with joy and good grace.

Connection Through Love

Joy cannot be found in separation,
Independence causes such deep pain.
Only through sharing and dedication,
Joining as one, can we all gain,
We are all the same.

The ego mind wants you to feel better than others,
Increasing isolation from the rest.
Yet joy can only come through loving your brothers,
Connectedness, peace, feeling truly blessed,
Through love we are all caressed.

To your ego you are always weak,
The mind it's tool, the illusion it's wealth.
Yet when you allow your Spirit to speak,
And work for your higher goal,
Pure potential, you free your *Self*, your Soul.

Your Spirit is constant, through your love,
Your mind is transient, in its fear.
Connect with your love and always give,
Banish fear, become a seer,
Through the illusion, your perception is clear.

Save Our Soul

Our fear runs deeper than the deepest ocean,
Our light shines brighter than the brightest sun,
Our thoughts control our destiny,
When all is said and done.

Our choices determine the path we take,
Our judgments limit our perception of life,
Our mind controls more than we can imagine,
It's the sole cause of our trouble and strife.

It's time to take responsibility,
For the power of our thoughts and mind,
Our ability to create good and bad,
The destruction we cause to our own kind.

We need to realize our own power,
And direct it for the good of all,
Connect with our fellow man,
And save our own Soul.

Forgiveness Is Hard To Do

Giving love is hard to do,
When we feel pain from another's action,
But pain is created from feeling weaker,
An internal distraction,
Our mind the speaker.

Letting go is hard to do,
When the pain in your mind feels so real,
Forgiveness is the only act,
It may seem quite surreal,
To ease the pain, it's a fact.

Forgiveness is so hard to do,
When you feel revenge is the deserving fate,
But harmful actions are never sweet,
Only more pain do they create,
And peace you can never meet.

Letting go is the only thing to do,
Recognizing your mind's struggle with others,
Only forgiveness can save the day,
Give love to your brothers,
Is the only way.

Breakthrough

Feeling tight, wound up and stressed,
My mind doesn't know what's best,
A figment of my imagination,
Driven by my interpretation.

Communication is so hard to do,
Cause no-one really thinks like you,
What they say isn't what they do,
They experience their world and so do you.

Stuck in my thoughts and pain,
Created by my mind again and again,
Ego driven fear and guilt,
Right and wrong, so damned important.

How can I breakthrough this mind space,
Find that special Spiritual place,
Know things for what they are,
See that I have come so far.

There is always more to be done,
People to test me, darken my sun,
Staying clear in mind is hard to do,
But it's something I must pursue.

Special Connection

When the feelings build, they become strong,
It's a hard state from which to get out,
Just want to scream and shout,
Don't want to be rational and understand,
Deserve to feel mad, head in the sand.

No desire to see what's going on,
My part in creating this destruction,
My thoughts, my feelings, my action,
Delivered with such perfection,
To maintain my dissatisfaction.

Not sure how it even started,
And no real reason to keep it going,
Except addiction to complaining and moaning,
There's got to be something better than this,
A place of light, happiness and bliss.

My mind maintains this sad illusion,
My heart and love can set it free,
Forgive all parties, including me,
Get back to what is real and true,
The special connection between me and you.

Heart & Mind

Uncertainty, discontent, frustration,
All the mind's orchestration.
Love, truth, joy,
All the heart deploys.
Knowing, lack, control,
All the mind's spoil.
Allowing, accepting, being,
The heart does the seeing.

The mind and heart two separate places,
Living in separate spaces,
Causing inner conflict and confusion,
The mind the servant, not buying the illusion.
To achieve true bliss and contentment,
The heart only can combat resentment.
Your passion is your fuel,
Your awareness your tool,
No longer a mind identified fool,
Love is your only goal.

Spiritual You

What brings relief to your mind,
Releases you.
What calms your *Self* and fills your Soul,
Graces you.
What generates passion in your heart,
Loves you.
What expresses compassion in your world,
Forgives you.
All these aspects of your life,
Spiritual YOU.

Inspiration & Faith

Inspiration is probably the most powerful energy within which change feels effortless and right to do. When you are feeling inspired you are on top of the world. Inspiration has a Spiritual quality to it. It is not tangible, yet you know it when you experience it. Inspiration will get you out of bed in the morning, sustain you through times of despair and engage your heart, mind and Soul. Inspirational people have had a massive impact across the world, some in a positive sense and others in a negative sense, depending on your perspective of course. Inspirational people such as Nelson Mandela, Martin Luther-King, Winston Churchill, Barack Obama, Adolf Hitler, Buddha, Jesus, and Mohammed have in some cases literally moved mountains. Their impact has been felt across time and space, resulting in major transformations of thinking and behaviours. Inspirational sports people and teams engage the nation and create desire and interest where none existed previously. The massive British cycling success in the early 21st Century raised the profile of cycling as an activity as well as a significant sport. The introduction of 20.20 cricket renewed interest in the sport that has outgrown the level of support received by the traditional Test cricket format.

If you feel inspired you will take action willingly and you will enjoy what you do. The secret is then to identify what inspires you, maintain your inspiration through the ups and downs, the highs the lows, successes and failures. To do this you need to be in tune with your reasons for doing what you do. If those reasons no longer give you the buzz they once did, your inspiration will not carry you through. Sometimes you will need to remind yourself of the good reasons for doing what you do. You need a purpose and ideally one that comes from within you.

Faith I describe as a sense of knowing without evidence. It is something you can believe in without seeing. Strongly aligned with trust, faith is essential in the development of positive mindsets and a healthy Spirit. Without faith your *Spiritual Self* will be overpowered, since your fear will be too strong and prevent it from expressing itself. Often people develop faith in things, systems, other people; things that are external to them. Be sure if you do this that what you are putting your faith in is there to truly support you. Putting your faith in God, as in your higher *Self*, is a safe bet. Putting your faith in other people and systems has to be done with an element of caution, since both are the subject of human fallibility and Ego influence, which may result in you feeling let down.

Learn to have faith in your *Self*, your higher *Self* and that you are on the right path for you. You cannot pray for success and hope that it comes to you, since this is not the way that your God works and is a misinterpretation that will leave you feeling frustrated; feeling that you have had faith and been let down. If you consult your God, seek guidance, forgiveness and give gratitude for what you have; your requests will be answered but not necessarily in the manner you were expecting. Remember the story of the old man stuck in his house in a flood. As the flood worsened he moved to the next floor and prayed for the flood to stop. A rescue boat came and he refused to move out of his house saying that God would save him. He moved to the next floor and prayed some more. A second rescue boat came and he still refused to budge. He moved to the roof still praying to God to stop the flood. The air rescue came and he refused to leave his house. He drowned and when he got to heaven he said to God, why didn't you rescue me? God replied, I sent you two boats and a helicopter, what more could I do? Have faith and also stay alert to the offerings that come your way.

Key Coaching Points:

* If you are no longer inspired by what you do, do something else.

* Reinventing yourself means finding your inspiration.

* Childhood dreams may still be your inspiration today, if they are then go for it.

* When your life has a purpose you will inspire others.

* Seek guidance not possessions and things.

* Have faith in your *Self*, not your ideal of perfection.

What You Love To Do

What is it that you love to do,
That really inspires you?
What gets you out of bed,
Creates a spark in your head?
What are you doing that makes time stand still,
What gives your heart a thrill?
Write a list, nothing missed,
Of all the things you love to do,
This is the essence of you.
And all the things that you don't like,
Get them to take a hike.
Unless there's value in what you are doing,
Pain, boredom and dullness are brewing.
To your *Self* you must be true,
And focus on what you love to do.

Having Faith In You

Having faith in you,
Is all that you can do,
Respect the world you are part of,
Know you are your inner God.

Having faith to trust your *Self*,
Your inner strength, your own true wealth,
Your higher *Self* your journey's guide,
In the universe you can confide.

For we are not alone in our lives,
Your Spirit connected to all that thrives,
At the highest level of your Soul,
All is one is your only goal.

In that place of connectedness,
Fear has no room or space,
Your faith, good grace, you are never alone,
Your comfort, your guide, your Spiritual home.

How Can You Not Believe?

How can you not believe,
How wonderful you are?
How can you not conceive,
You are a precious star?

Your light that shines so bright,
Of which you have no sight,
Is burning deep inside,
No longer there to hide.

Your spark deep inside your Soul,
Your inner love, your desire and fuel,
Let it out for all to see,
Be the you, you want to be.

Live The Life You Want Today

Engaging in how things feel,
Is the only thing that's truly real.
We can know through intellect and mind,
But still not change our habits, still blind.
To the experiences we need in life,
Let go of your troubles and strife.
Unless you engage at an emotional level,
You cannot change, your mind will prevail.
Pain will still reside in you,
And influence all that you do.
Keep doing things all the same,
Even though conceptually you may know,
Nothing will change, you cannot grow.
Emotions are our fuel, good or bad,
Repression will only leave you sad.
Expressing your *Self* is the only way,
To live the life you want today.

Awareness Of You

When you start to become aware,
You can easily feel so scared.
You will see there's lots to do,
When you look closely at you.

All your flaws there in your face,
You must accept with good grace.
Allow your Spirit to guide you now,
On your journey, trust you know how.

Your inner wisdom does reside,
In your awareness deep inside.
You must be brave as you go there,
Overcome your fear and idea of what's fair.

Trust in your higher sense of what's true,
Knowing what's real and believing in you.
Overcome your mortal being,
Open your inner eyes and start seeing.

Your Fun

Where does your fun come from?
Is it what you think or what you have done?
What is it that brightens your day?
What do you do in your life that's play?
Where is the child in you today?

So serious in all that you do,
No creative expression, nothing that's new.
So black and white,
Only wrong and right,
Where is your light?

There is a child in all of us,
That needs to express, be curious.
Innocent, no fear of fun and laughs,
Simple, a pure light that parts,
The sadness. It's the joy in you that lasts.

Be Inspired

Love yourself and who you are,
Be inspired you've come so far,
And what you've forgotten along the way,
Will come back to you in the light of day.

As you trust your inner guide,
And don't just follow the rules that blind,
Come to know what faith is for you,
Your sense of what is really true.

Close to your God on high,
Your inner strength, your chance to fly,
It's always there within your whole,
Your light, pure love, your Soul.

Reach it, touch it, it is your grace,
Ever lasting love, unwavering faith,
This is who you really are,
Be inspired you've come so far.

Be True

If you feel no passion in what you do,
You need to find something new,
Be true to what inspires you.

Don't let fear hold you back,
In this life you must not crack,
For time you lack.

Don't accept pain as the only way,
Striving, fighting, no time for play,
Living a life so grey.

With possibilities all around,
Your expression, choice abound,
A better life to be found.

Release your passion through what you do,
Do only what inspires you,
One love, one life; be true.

What's Right for You

When you feel inspired you will do,
Exactly what is right for you,
Your life will be full of joy and love,
Faith your guide, nothing to be afraid of.

Your heart and Soul so bright,
Your love shines pure light,
You are free at last,
Your life's a blast.

When feeling inspired,
You are never tired,
Because you always do,
What's right for you.

Faith Restored

Through your faith,
You feel content,
All you receive,
Is heaven sent.

No striving for more,
No feeling of lack,
You have all you need,
No looking back.

No pain, no loss,
No guilt, no shame,
Inadequacy,
Is not part of your game.

Your Spirit strong,
Faith restored,
Content with your *Self*,
Your life you applaud.

Your Life the Theme

Love and affection,
Feel your connection,
To your Spirit and Soul,
You are whole.

On your own,
But never alone,
The seed is sown,
You have grown.

Never doubt,
What you are about,
You are always free,
To simply be.

Your light shines bright,
Your inner sight,
Your passion, your dream,
Your life the theme.

Looking In the Mirror

When you look in the mirror, don't like what you see,
You're not looking at you; you are looking through me,
Your ego mind, that keeps you blind,
For your real beauty it cannot see.

When you look in the mirror and love what you see,
You're looking at you and not through me,
Your Spirit so pure, your Soul secure,
Your beauty is there for you to see.

Choose the lens through which you see,
Your Ego blind, your Spirit free,
Be on your side, your own true guide,
And see the best that you can be.

Engage Your Heart's Fire

The child in you,
So pure and true,
Full of fun and joy.
Must be released,
To free the beast,
The adult life destroys.

Keep in touch with fun,
Allow in the sun,
Create the life you desire.
Let your child out,
Just scream and shout,
Engage your heart's fire.

Your Spiritual Self

Why criticize when you can praise?
Why be dull when you can amaze?
Allow your brilliance to shine through,
Express the love that's deep within you.
Open your heart, see the good that's out there,
In love with your *Self*, your deepest affair.
Your bright light shining, to the world you give,
Through your *Spiritual Self* is the only way to live.

You'll Always Get Through

When life feels like an uphill struggle,
Swimming against the tide,
When you feel so stuck, out of luck,
In your Spirit you must confide.

When there's no direction with what you do,
The value and love are gone,
No passion you feel, no appeal,
In your faith you must be strong.

Give yourself time to review your choices,
And find the inspiration you need.
Of time and space, and good grace,
And gratitude you feed.

Because no matter how bad it gets,
How low you feel you could go,
With Spirit and faith, and good grace,
You'll always get through... you'll grow.

F.A.I.T.H.

Forgiveness is the gift you're given,
Acceptance the challenge you face,
Intuition is the guide you need,
Trust is your journey's fate,
Humility is the lesson you learn,
FAITH is the key to your Soul's grace.

Living In Faith

Faith is something bigger than yourself,
You cannot hear, or feel, or see,
A sense of knowing you cannot define,
In faith you can believe.

A higher force watching over you,
From which you can feel strong,
Connecting all to live as one,
In faith you can belong.

You Saved My Life

I know you saved my life today,
When you smiled at me.
You gave me hope that love exists,
That one day it would set me free.

I know you saved my life today,
When you spoke kindly to me.
Whispering softly inside my head,
Giving me faith I could be.

I didn't think you'd come to me,
Didn't believe it could be true.
But I heard your voice, saw your face,
That's how I know it's you.

You were there when I needed you most,
You answered my call,
Saved my life again and again,
My God, my saviour, my all.

Recommended Reading

Achieving Peak Performance In Tennis by Helen K Emms

Ageless Body, Timeless Mind by Deepak Chopra

Anatomy of the Spirit: The Seven Stages of Power and Healing by Caroline Myss Ph.D

A New Earth by Eckhart Tolle

Conversations With God Neale Donald Walsch

Defy Gravity by Caroline Myss

Destructive Emotions by Daniel Goleman

Feel the Fear & Do It Anyway: How to Turn Your Fear and Indecision into Confidence and Action by Susan Jeffers

Inspiration Your Ultimate Calling by Dr Wayne W. Dyer

Molecules of Emotion: Why You Feel the Way You Feel by Candace B. Pert Ph.d

Power Freedom and Grace by Deepak Chopra

Power vs Force by David R Hawkins

Sacred Contracts by Caroline Myss

Take me to Truth: Undoing the Ego by Nouk Sanchez and Tomas Vieira

The Biology of Belief: Unleashing the Power of Consciousness, Matter and Miracles by Bruce Lipton PhD

✓ **The Book of Secrets** by Deepak Chopra

The Brain that Changes Itself: Stories of Personal Triumph from the Frontiers of Brain Science by Norman Doidge

✓ **The Celestine Prophecy** by James Redfield

The Holographic Universe by Michael Talbot

The Law of Attraction: How to Make it Work for You by Esther & Jerry Hicks

✓ **The Power of Now** by Eckhart Tolle

The Psychology of Emotion by K.T. Strongman

✓ **The Way of the Peaceful Warrior** by Dan Millman

✓ **Why People Don't Heal & How They Can** by Caroline Myss

✓ **Your Body Speaks Your Mind: Understanding How Your Emotions and Thoughts Affect You Physically** by Deb Shapiro

About the Author

Helen Emms is the Author of *Achieving Peak Performance in Tennis*. She has coached and inspired thousands of people throughout the UK to unleash their potential. From her experiences in the Army, coaching sports teams and training soldiers to cope in the highest pressure situations through to her role in Industry, developing high performing teams, Helen knows how to tap into each person's inner motivation for success. Her own insatiable appetite for learning and passion for discovering new ways to work with her clients has led Helen to achieve the highest level of qualification and practical experience as a Psychologist, Clinical Hypnotherapist, Certified Trainer of NLP, EFT Practitioner, Reiki Master and Peak Performance Coach. Helen is now currently supporting the UK's top Tennis Academy and works with coaches, players and their parents to achieve their highest potential.

If you would like more information about how Helen can help you please visit her website at www.spiritinsport.co.uk.

"Live your life through your Spirit and Soul"

Index

Review, 11, 60, 62-3, 142-3, 151, 192

Sabotage, 24, 100
Self, 1, 3, 20, 23, 25-6, 31, 34-5, 37, 55, 58, 64, 68, 72, 80, 82-3, 90, 94, 97, 103, 113, 116, 124, 126, 128, 130, 132, 139, 142, 153-5, 158, 166, 168, 174, 176-9, 181, 187, 191, *Also See* Spiritual Self
Self-esteem, 130
Soul, 26, 37, 58-9, 84, 97-8, 103-4, 120, 130, 160-1, 165-6, 168-9, 174-5, 179-80, 184, 186, 188-89, 193, 196
Spirit, 1, 5, 26, 68, 104, 118, 155-6, 160-1, 163, 166-8, 176, 179, 182, 187-9, 192, 196-7
Spiritual Self, 1-3, 20, 34, 36, 90, 113, 132, 142, 153, 155, 176, 191

Succeed. *See* Success
Success, 24, 27, 30, 34, 40, 43, 45, 59, 67, 69, 71, 80, 89, 99, 100, 101-5, 108-9, 111, 118, 120, 122, 126, 128-31, 136, 140-1, 166, 175-6, 196

Talent, 1-2, 59, 66, 68-70, 75-7, 104, 110-1, 159
Thinking, 2-3, 6, 14, 16-22, 28-9, 32, 34, 36, 42, 47, 70, 75, 78-80, 113, 130, 132-3, 139, 141, 144, 175
Thoughts, 4, 6-9, 14, 16-7, 19-25, 28, 31-2, 35-6, 39-41, 46, 50-2, 56, 65, 77, 94, 122, 133, 142, 169, 171-2

Uncertainty, 27, 47, 65-7, 79, 80-1, 108, 173

ACHIEVING
Peak Performance in Tennis
Helen K Emms

Tennis should be fun. It should be about experiencing effortless flow as you challenge yourself and achieve the success you want on court. Instead though, for many players their joy of the game is shattered because of failure, a lack of confidence, heart ache and the disappointment of unrealised expectations.

Achieving Peak Performance in Tennis gives you a comprehensive and new understanding of your mental game including psychological and energetic influences that you will not have considered before now. Read this book and learn how to successfully overcome the instinctive drives that limit your game and how to raise your awareness to achieve your highest potential. Bring the joy of tennis back into your game by discovering how to:

- Deal with pressure, perfectionism and expectations
- Build self-esteem, self-belief and confidence
- Develop emotional control, resilience and mental strength
- Stop trying so hard and get better results
- Turn failure into success and much, much more!

Achieving Peak Performance in Tennis is essential sports psychology reading for Tennis Coaches, Parents and Players who want to unleash the full power of their mind and energy system to win more!

"FASCINATNG, enthralling, transformational.
Everyone involved in tennis should read this."
Matt Willcocks, Tennis Director
Gosling International High Performance Centre

Lightning Source UK Ltd.
Milton Keynes UK
03 June 2010

155031UK00001B/21/P